Praise for
There Is No Hell
and for Linnie Thomas from clients and friends

"We all have curiosity about the dimension beyond this physical life. Do we have a soul? Are there ghosts? What happens to us after we die? Linnie Thomas is an extraordinary energy healer, psychic, and medium who has been to the other side. Through her fascinating and illuminating stories, she will take you on a journey to explore the mystery questions. I believe!"

Jean Slatter, Founder of the
Higher Guidance Life Coach program and
Author of ***Hiring the Heavens***

"Your writing has really helped to unlock some of my own grief. The experiences that you report are much like other accounts I've read. The proposition that we 'contracted' in advance with full foreknowledge—that we freely chose and designed our current Life School curriculum, is not new to me. But for whatever reasons—that I know and respect you personally—or your accessible writing style—or that the time was right, I took it in at a new level. I trusted and embraced the knowledge that everything is happening with purpose that was welcomed by all participants, albeit on another superior plane."

Steve Fulmer

"I thoroughly enjoyed reading this book. Information often comes to us at just the right time, and this was one of those times for me. Your experiences validated and affirmed my own. A very good read."

Peggy Mullett, Founder of
Peaceable Kingdom Animal Therapy

"I slowly and purposely read this book to savor the thoughts and new ideas that I was seeing, and I thoroughly enjoyed it. It is fascinating. So much to take in and think about; I have much to mull over. Just like the last word in the book: Wow!"

Terri Pender

"Linnie is a gifted healer, mentor, and teacher. She has a calm and reassuring presence as she teaches her classes. I had spent a day and a half trying to master one particularly vital healing technique. On the final day of the weekend class, Linnie came over and just held her hands over mine to help guide me, and reassured me that I could indeed do it. In that moment, everything aligned and I felt what I had spent 36 hours trying to learn.

Linnie also helped me with a spirit in a home that I had just purchased. I knew the spirit was there, but had neither the experience nor skill to help move it to the light. Linnie released the spirit and I was able to move into my new home feeling that it was clean and ready for my energy."

Jamie Marthaler, RN

"Linnie Thomas is my role model for visiting and comforting those less fortunate than herself."

Christine Sorenson

"Linnie is a teacher in our community filled with wisdom, strength, and light. We thank her for gifting all of us with the knowledge from her soul. There are no words in the dictionary to describe how amazing she is."

Janna Moll, MSN, HTCP/1, LMT
Founder of **Energy Medicine Specialists**

"Linnie Thomas is a real thought leader in the field of energy medicine and healing and a pioneer in bringing visibility and viability to the field of energy medicine. She is able to view the industry from a higher perspective and share a worldview of the effectiveness and importance of biofield therapies with the public and practitioners.

In her book, *The Encyclopedia of Energy Medicine*, she provides comprehensive descriptions of the most widely used and professional energy modalities, giving people who are seeking alternative therapies a place to explore and understand what is available. In *Laws Governing Energy Medicine Practitioners*, Linnie supports and highlights the importance of practicing legally in the energy medicine field.

Both books are valuable reference manuals that help spread awareness of energy healing therapies and further the care and rights of individuals to be treated and viewed as whole in body, mind, emotions, and spirit. This book promises to be another best-seller."

Lisa Mentgen-Gordon
CEO/Visionary, **Healing Touch Program™**

"Linnie Thomas speaks and writes her truth. She is love in action."

Tennie Bottomly

There Is No Hell

Linnie Thomas

Copyright © 2018 by Linnie Thomas

Cover/Author photos by Jaya Thompson of JayaVision Photography
Interior Design by Fine Wordworking

All rights reserved. No part of this publication may be used or reproduced in any manner whatsoever without written permission, except in the case of brief quotations embodied in critical articles and reviews. For further information, please contact the author.

 The author of this book does not dispense medical advice nor prescribe the use of any technique as a form of treatment for physical, emotional, or medical problems without the advice of a physician, either directly or indirectly. The intent of the author is only to offer information to help you in your quest for emotional, physical, and spiritual wellbeing. In the event that you use any of the information in this book for yourself, the author and the publisher assume no responsibility for your actions.

Published by Ellinwood Publishing

Library of Congress-in-Publication Data

Thomas, Linnie 1946 –

There is no hell/Linnie Thomas

ISBN-13: 978-1987521122
ISBN-10: 1987521129

  1. Hell

Printed in the United States of America
First Printing

10 9 8 7 6 5 4 3 2 1

Dedicated to
Steve Fulmer
*in gratitude for his many acts of kindness
and unceasing devotion to helping others*

Dedicated posthumously to
Chris Korsgaard
who wanted answers.

CONTENTS

Introduction	xi
Acknowledgments	xxi
1 In the Beginning	1
2 The Quest	5
3 My First Experience with a Transition	13
4 Another Unusual Experience	19
5 My Stepfather's Transition	23
6 My Dad	27
7 The Continued Search	37
8 My Own Near-Death Experience	53
9 A Student Makes His Transition	59
10 A Client's Transition	63
11 Soul Fragments and Other Entities in the Energy Field	69

12	A New Experience	81
13	The Professor's House	87
14	A Miscarriage	93
15	Two Ghosts	99
16	My Mother-in-Law's Transition	103
17	Roseburg	109
18	A Dog's Transition	115
19	Some Other Experiences	121
20	A Mortgage Problem	125
21	The Lawyer	131
22	Grief	137
23	There Is No Hell	145
24	A Late Addition	159
Also by Linnie Thomas		161
About the Author		163

Introduction

*Remember that you are not alone in the world.
You depend on a thousand creatures that sustain the
fabric of your life. The mirror of your heart is permeated
with a multitude of images. Your soul is like a feather
carried by the winds. But much more is still needed
before you see yourself as you are.*

FAOUZI SKALI

My father summed it up very nicely. "I'm not afraid of dying," he said to me one day. "It's the process of getting there that bothers me." I agree with him. I have requested that when my time comes, I would like to have a nice little heart attack and leave the planet. I am not interested in any of this cancer nonsense, or worse, dementia. When it's time to go home, let's make it sweet and simple.

So many people are terrified of dying. Our society supports the fear. Advertisements, especially concerning health and beauty, encourage people to hide the fact that they are aging. For some reason, we are taught to hide our true age. It's as if there is something wrong with taking eighty, ninety, or even a hundred trips around the sun.

The prevalence of dementia has added to the dislike of growing older. Fortunately, not everyone gets dementia. A great many people stay clear headed until they take their last breath. Many work long past retirement age, not because they have to, but because they love what they do. Having a reason to get up in the morning is important. A life well lived can be long or short. It really doesn't matter.

What makes a life well lived? Each person has a different point of view. I like to think I will arrive at the pearly gates, tattered and worn with a grin on my face, announcing, "Wow! What a ride! Let's do it again!"

I wanted this book to be of comfort for people who have loved ones facing death or are about to make a transition of their own. I like the term, *transition*, since I firmly believe we don't stop when the body quits. Instead we move on to another place. Most reincarnate. We have choice.

Having choice is what it is all about. We live on a free will planet. I don't know about the rest of the galaxy, or even the universe, and I really don't care. It's this lifetime that is important to me. People have asked me about free will and what does it mean. Animals act and react to events

INTRODUCTION

in their lives based on instincts. They don't have the choices we do. Instinct runs the show. Dogs and cats do have very different personalities, but they also act and react in specific ways. For example, cats play with their prey, dogs do not. Some birds mate for life, others do not. It depends upon their species and they don't have choice.

Humans always have choice. We choose our parents before we arrive on the planet. We choose potential circumstances, too. We make a lot of choices all through our lifetimes. I read once the average American now makes more decisions in one day than he or she did in one year over a hundred years ago. We're busy.

I had planned on writing strictly about death and dying. However, books have a way of writing themselves, even nonfiction. I start out with a given topic and the next thing I know I have expanded into the next county. This book is no exception. Other stuff kept creeping in. I wonder, at times, who is actually writing this book? My life-long quest to know why we are here seems to have run the show. Abilities that until now I have kept hidden, secret to all but a few trusted friends and family, suddenly showed up and went down on paper. Oogh, do I really want to do that? I have choice, remember? I gave in to the encouragement. No one forced me, and instincts certainly had no part in it.

My guides insisted I write about who and what I am. My answer to that was, *"Oh crap!"* From time to time I can see ghosts. How weird is that? I came from a family where reason and logic ruled our lives. My father and his father were civil engineers who designed railroad bridges. My mother's father was a lawyer. Anything at all woo-woo just didn't happen.

I grew up sheltered in a community of innocent kids a lot like me. Looking back, I can see hints of family troubles. Nobody ever talked about it. When one of my classmates committed suicide, it came as a huge shock. Of course, we didn't have counselors to come in and help us with our grief like students do today. We persevered and life went on.

I had a mentor. He entered my life as coworker of my first husband. The two of them were going hunting together and the coworker felt I should meet him before sharing a potentially dangerous sport with my husband. At first sight, I knew there was something different about the man. My husband and I talked about him for years afterward. We still do from time to time.

My mentor once told me I had reached a point in my life where I needed to make a choice: I could choose to be a telepath or an empath. I really didn't know what an empath was. My mentor explained. A telepath would be able to know what a person was thinking. An empath would know what a person or animal was feeling. Of the two, an empath was the more powerful. That didn't make much sense at the time. I thought about it for several days. and the next time I saw him I told him I had chosen empath. I still didn't understand the difference, but empath felt right to me.

He told me that I was only recognizing what I truly was. In the 1970s being a telepath was attractive. We had television shows like *Star Trek* and movies like *Star Wars* encouraging us to go beyond ourselves. I wanted to know why he offered me the choice. He said it was an opportunity for me to choose my heart's longing rather than the popular myths surrounding us at the time. You see? Choice.

I met with him often for several years until he died. I was trying so hard to figure out the purpose of the universe and why we are here. He introduced me to the possibility that there is more to life than what I could see, hear, or touch. His stories fascinated me. For the most part, they were just stories. I couldn't prove any of them, but I loved hearing them just the same

I turned away from what I would call a normal life when I began to study energy medicine, which I prefer to call biofield therapy. Biofield therapy is the more correct terminology. Hands-on healing is a therapy not a medicine, if you go by the dictionary definitions. When people ask me what I do, I like to say I am a biofield therapist and I work with the human energy field. It's an accurate description.

I've written books on the subject of biofield therapy. I am a Healing Touch Certified Instructor and Practitioner and have a thriving private practice. While learning a clearing technique, one of my instructors mentioned that the technique could be used to clear congested energy from a building as well as an energy field. I didn't think much about it at the time, but later found it to be a very useful tool in a number of situations having nothing to do with the human energy field.

When I took the Healing Touch for Animals Level 1 class, I gained a new perspective. Animals love receiving energy work. They will present the area of their body that hurts to the practitioner with no thought as to whether it will work or not. They appear to have no doubts. When the energy work is complete the animal walks away. I love working with horses. I don't know who is healing who when it comes to horses. For the most part, they are very loving animals. Their energy fields extend out about twenty feet. All living things have a distinct energy field.

As do inanimate things. The ocean has a different *feel* to it when compared to a lake or river. Mountains *feel* different than prairies. Rocks made of specific minerals *feel* different

Introduction

from rocks made of other materials. Inanimate objects can carry the emotions and feelings from events that occur in their presence.

Scientists are now saying that mass is nothing more than condensed energy. Everything is energy all vibrating at a myriad of levels. That each thing, living or inanimate, has its own field comes as no surprise. To take on other vibrations carrying trauma or joy by plants or inanimate objects can and does happen.

I would not have thought inanimate objects had energy fields. I was thinking about this when I remembered an event that happened many years ago and has been repeated in various ways since that time. I lovingly call my first husband my *wusband*. He is still a good friend even though we separated a long time ago. It was the week of Halloween and we bought a brown bag full of orange and black jelly beans. My wusband liked the black ones, I did not. I found I could reach into the bag without looking and pull out an orange jelly bean for me. It felt different from the black ones. When my wusband asked for a black one, nine times out of ten, I would pull out a black one for him.

I cannot tell you how I knew the difference. I don't know if I felt an energetic difference, or that my skin recognized the difference between the two colors. I have played the game a few times since then. I have played it with different kinds of chocolate and even checker pieces. Some days I would get it right every time and other days the colors I picked came up at random. I am not consistent, which annoys me.

One of my favorite stories about plants comes from the book, *The Secret Life of Plants* by Peter Tompkins and Christopher Bird. A lie detector examiner, Cleve Backster, placed two plants in a room and connected one plant to a galvanometer. It recorded a steady vibration emanating from the plant. He then wrote out instructions on six pieces of paper and placed each sheet of paper in an envelope and sealed it. Six people participated in the experiment. One of the pieces of paper contained instructions for the recipient to destroy the plant not connected to the galvanometer. The person receiving the envelope containing those instructions did as requested. The galvanometer recorded wild reactions from the unharmed plant. Each time the person who did the dastardly deed entered the room, the plant reacted. It stayed calm whenever anyone else walked into the room.

Maybe there will come a day when a plant or rock can testify at a trial because we will have learned to communicate with such things.

As you read this book, you'll find you are in for an experience. Many people will think I am full of beans. Some will feel like they have come home. I really don't care. It's up to you to decide how you want to think about what I have written, not me. I wouldn't take that freedom away from you for anything. I couldn't. It's the way things are. And we all agreed to abide by the rules when we came here. From time to time I find those rules annoying.

I have memories of walking through walls, for example. When I hit my head on something, I often wish I hadn't agreed to the rules that govern this planet. It would have been nice to pass my head through the mass of whatever I bumped into and saved myself the pain of the experience. And gravity always works. It's just the way of it. I know that time is more than the fourth dimension. It doesn't limit us on the other side of the veil.

I have had the pleasure of working with many guides throughout the years. Oreg is my favorite and the one I rely on when working with a healing client.

Guides can change. This came as a surprise to me. I thought we were assigned to, or make an agreement with one or more specific spiritual beings before we are born, and that we would always have that guide or guides as long as we live. Not so. Different levels of awareness require different guides. I do not know why this is. I had always assumed those on the other side know everything. Another big surprise. They don't.

Oreg first announced his presence when I opened a professional healing practice. His critiques were highly valuable to me. I always call him in for consultation when doing healing work. I have also come to rely on him for everyday advice concerning events in my current life.

He once told me he had over three hundred beings available, each specializing in various problems such as cancer, relationships, or even financial matters. He contacts the guides of my clients before I see them. The client's needs determine which specialists Oreg requests.

I thought about dedicating this book to him. However, guides don't have egos and he told me he didn't need to be singled out that way. Still, I owe him a debt of gratitude. I can't thank him enough for all his help.

Acknowledgments

I wish to thank the following people:

Dayana Patterson for her endless patience with me while editing this book and all her valuable suggestions.

AMAG for talking me into writing this book.

Kathryn Stillings for convincing me this work is not just a figment of my imagination.

Joyce Strahn for asking me to clear the first house of ghosts.

Steve Fulmer for helping me to understand grief.

There Is No Hell

1

In the Beginning

*There is a place I can find answers. There is a place I see who I am. And in this place, life's full of wonder.
I'll meet you there…*

JAYNEE THORNE

I first noticed I had abilities others didn't when my children were little. My wusband and I took the children on a road trip across America to visit relatives and friends on the East Coast. One of the places we visited was Mount Vernon. Mind you, this was a long time ago. We were free to walk all over the grounds, and we did.

At one point, we came across a dark and frightening place that I remember as having possibly been a large outdoor oven, presumably used for cooking whole pigs and other large chunks of meat. At that time, I knew nothing about energy work, angels, guides, ghosts, or spooks. I sensed a feeling of such intense, uncomfortable energy coming from the oven that I backed away and wouldn't let my children anywhere near it.

We explored other areas and later came back to the oven or whatever it was. I wanted to know if I felt the same sensation or if I were imagining things. If anything, the dark feelings intensified. My memory is sketchy here. I remember it as an opening in the side of a little rise. I do remember the inside as being black. No sunlight entered that opening. I felt hatred, pain, shame, misery, and other unpleasantries emanating from that place. To this day, I wonder what happened there to create such dark feelings.

Later on, we went to Arlington National Cemetery. I was very impressed with the place and felt a great reverence for the people buried there. We saw the changing of the guard at the Tomb of the Unknown Soldier. To quote a friend of mine, "It was awesome."

However, I was surprised when we got to the gravesite of John F. Kennedy. All the other graves had residual energy coming from each grave. At his grave, I felt nothing. I don't think he is buried there. I feel it is a token grave for the nation to honor our fallen president.

This feeling intensified after we drove around Cape Cod

and visited Hyannis Port, Massachusetts. We drove down a street that went by the Kennedy Compound. In the center of the street was a little garden with a statue in the middle of it. I don't remember much about the garden or the statue, but I do remember hearing a man crying. He mourned for his lost life and the work he had to leave unfinished. The sadness of it has stayed with me all these years later.

I took these and a few other experiences seriously, but I didn't know what to do about it. We didn't have the Internet. I felt uncomfortable about sharing what I saw and felt. I wasn't sure if I believed in ghosts and other spiritual stuff. Then a strange thing happened. I decided I would learn about witchcraft. We lived on a mountaintop in Oregon. Our driveway was about a third of a mile long and was shared by other property owners.

One of the property owners wanted to sell a chunk of land bordering the driveway. Actually, his land ended in the middle of the driveway and a piece of land that we owned covered the other half of the driveway at that point. The neighbor's land didn't sell right away. He decided to cut down some trees on the land hoping to make it more attractive to a potential buyer. We loved the trees and didn't like to see them cut down.

I put a curse on any machinery that brought harm to the trees and that property. I didn't know what I was doing, but it seemed like a good idea at the time. He quit cutting down trees shortly after that. I don't know if he had any equipment problems or not.

My wusband had taken an interest in a gal where he worked. He wanted to marry her and you know what that meant. Anyway, one day she came to visit and I wasn't there. She got about twenty feet down the driveway when the motor fell out of her car. I haven't touched witchcraft since that event and have no desire to ever do so again.

I decided to go a different direction.

2

The Quest

It is not the answer that enlightens, but the question.
Découvertes

Actually, the quest began in the seventh grade. I loved my seventh-grade teacher. We stayed friends until she made her transition several years ago. She had a marvelous way of introducing us to new ideas. She read to us every day after lunch. She loved science fiction and I grew to love it that year as well. The first book she read aloud to the class was about mushroom people who lived on a planet exactly opposite of ours from the sun. Therefore, it was never seen or detected. My mind liked to play with that idea. I have heard similar stories about a mysterious planet on the other side of the sun. To my disappointment, astronomers have since proved that possibility to be false.

The second book she read to us, *Between Planets*, by Robert Heinlein, really played with my imagination. I went on to read every Heinlein book I could get my hands on. At some point, I transferred my attention to Andre Norton. Many of Norton's books dealt with advanced cultures, long gone, leaving hints about why we are here and what life is all about. I was always disappointed because Norton never actually came out and said anything worthwhile. It was all hints and possibilities.

My ultimate quest became, *"Why am I here?"* which eventually segued into, *"Why are we here?"* Fantasy had not really come into its own in the late 1960s, and early '70s. I had to make do with science fiction. I found a short story in a sci/fi magazine that really set the stage for my quest. In the story, cats had taken over as the lead sentient beings. One cat became curious as to why the human race had died off. For years, the cat searched for the origins of the human race on various planets. At last the cat found a reference to a planet called Earth. Many cat cultures thought Earth was a myth. He searched the star maps until he finally found its location.

Once there, the cat poked around in several old libraries on Earth with no results. However, one highly restricted library refused him admittance in spite of his credentials. After much effort, he managed to sneak into the library. It contained only one book. He opened the book to a page marked by a ribbon. He glanced at other pages to see what they said. They were all blank.

The marked page read, "There is no reason for living." It didn't really ring my chimes at that time. I felt uncomfortable whenever I thought about it. However, the idea has stayed with me until this day. The quest for the reason for living began in earnest after I read that story.

I looked in two directions: religion and more science fiction. Actually, I looked to science as well. I decided to study nuclear physics as a way of finding God. I knew of other students studying either nuclear physics or astronomy with the same goal. It didn't work out very well for me, as I had a wee bit of a bother about the math. I did well in math in high school, but college math was a foreign language.

So that didn't work. Science fiction hinted at answers, but never really came out and said this is it. That left religion. Now religion was a bother. My folks took us kids to Sunday school every week. I never thought to question why they didn't go to church at the same time. We moved a lot. We kids attended Sunday school at whatever church was nearby every week. Even at an early age, I asked questions that my teachers couldn't answer, or I challenged their beliefs, not knowing I was doing so.

I could not accept a God who sent people to Hell simply because they had never heard of Jesus. I had trouble with good and evil, too. One church said one thing and another said something different, even though they both professed to be Christian. The only answer I ever got about why are we here was that if we were good, when we died we got to sit at the feet of God and adore Him, singing His praises forever. That sounded pretty boring, both to me and to God.

Some of my cousins were Catholic and that religion fascinated me. Most of what I knew about Catholicism was hearsay. I attended mass a couple of times with my cousins. I thought it was magical. I loved the idea that I couldn't eat before mass and that I had to cover my hair with a hat or scarf. This was before Vatican II. It was ceremony that I liked and is something missing in today's culture. Ceremony creates a feeling of togetherness. It also symbolizes seriousness in whatever is going on.

Eventually my answers came, little bit by little bit. I would get a hint here and another there. It frustrated me no end. Hundreds of answers came my way from well-meaning people. Those answers made no sense most of the time. Either that or they simply didn't say enough.

As the years passed, I noticed the answers to the same

question changed. I found this annoying. Truth is truth, isn't it? My mentor told me that what is true for one person is not true for another. Truth itself exists, but is not necessarily expressed as being true. I found this confusing.

Along came a little company called PSI World, Inc. I have had many blessings in my life and PSI World is one of them. In January of 1978, my wusband talked me into attending the PSI Basic class. They are still teaching that class and I have gone back many times over the years. Once you have taken the class, you can audit it for free for the rest of your life. Thomas D. Willhite, founder of the class, believed returning students added value to the subject matter. I highly recommend taking the class. I learn something new each time I go.

The first day of class I noticed a sign behind the facilitator's head that read, TO THINK IS TO CREATE. In my loftiness, I thought, "Well, if you have a problem and think about it for a while, you can come up with possible solutions. I've got this class nailed."

The following day another sign showed up that read, THOUGHTS ARE THINGS. This was getting better. After all a thought is a noun, therefore it could be called a thing, which reaffirmed my original feelings about the class.

Until the third day, that is. A new sign showed up on the wall. This one said, IF YOU DON'T LIKE WHERE YOU'RE AT,

CHANGE YOUR THINKING. I realized I didn't have a clue in the closet what they were talking about.

Another quest came about with this new concept. How did my thinking influence my world and the events in it?

The facilitators of the class were the first ones to introduce me to the concept of each of us being totally responsible for our lives. I wasn't ready to hear that at the time. However, the idea never left me.

I didn't want to take personal responsibility for my life. I didn't want to admit I caused the mess I found myself in. I was a very unhappy camper until I finally figured out that if I took responsibility, it meant I could change my own world. That gave me a freedom I didn't know existed. I had liberty! I didn't know what to do with it yet, but I had hope from then on.

Which brought me back to the concept, "To think is to create." Could I possibly be the creator of my own world? If I am creating my own world, and everyone else is creating their own world, it seemed to me there would be a lot of conflict and some would override others. Let's face it, we do have conflict on this planet. That's what makes it interesting and fun.

Actually, it is that simple and yet not quite that simple. We blend our worlds together like a weaver fabricates cloth. An example of that is when the thought of a friend you haven't seen in a while wafts through your mind. A few minutes later the phone rings and guess who is on the other end of the line?

Even though we are connected at the source, we are each a unique and wonderful creature. We are not all one though. We are autonomous. Yet as we create our own worlds, we interact with each other to fill the needs of those interwoven worlds. The individual cells in your body act according to their own functions and needs. Together they form your whole body.

That's a lot to think about.

3

My First Experience with a Transition

*Life after death is the elephant in the living room,
the one that we are not supposed to notice.
Our culture, which prides itself on its open-mindedness
and candor, shows an intense antipathy to facing
the greatest of all human questions.*

DINESH D'SOUZA

I was eighteen years old when my grandfather died. His death was traumatic for the family. It came unexpectedly. We had a couple of days warning when he had a stroke, from which his chosen method of recovery was to leave us.

My father refused to allow my brother and me to see

Grandpa before he died. I think Dad was trying to shield us from what he thought was one of the saddest events in life. Recently, the thought came to me that he may not have wanted to answer questions for which he had no answers. Little did he know that in later years I would work with the dead and the dying. Be that as it may, I was unprepared for my reaction during the events immediately following Grandpa's death.

We visited the funeral home the day before the funeral, a couple of days after Grandpa died. Most of the immediate family came that day. Aunts and uncles, a few cousins, my parents and my step-grandmother were all there. We are not a big family. My grandmother did not come that day. She was not well liked as she had some mental problems, which brought about a divorce from my grandfather. I don't remember her ever attending any family events other than an occasional dinner, or Christmas with just my parents, my brother and me.

I had never been in a funeral home before. I did not expect a bright and cheerful atmosphere. Pale yellow paint covered the walls. Colorful flowers adorned the tables decorating the entry way and reception room. I thought it looked very nice, not at all sad.

The people there spoke to us in quiet solemn tones. This was not a place to play tag or shout for the pure joy of living. I got the message, loud and clear, that we were there for a very sad occasion, and the funeral home personnel would help us get through it as best they could.

We toured the facilities. They had a private room for the family separate from the main chapel. This was a time before memorial services became popular and now, memorial services have segued into celebrations of life which suits me much better.

The subject of my grandmother came up. What were we to do with her? My step- grandmother did not want to be in the same room with her, so the funeral home people divided us. My parents and my brother and I were to sit in a curtained-off area to one side of the chapel with my grandmother. The rest of the family were to sit in the private room meant for grieving family members. I guess it wasn't considered proper to see family members cry.

I don't think my father liked being separated from the rest of the family, but he felt it was the duty of a son to support his mother. My mother didn't like it at all, but she didn't fuss about it in front of the rest of the family. We heard about it later at home.

I looked forward to the funeral. I saw it as a great time to be with my cousins and eat lots of food, especially cookies and other dessert type things that make up a family feast.

We entered the building on the day of the funeral. It was so bright I thought the sun was shining right through the roof. No one commented on how bright the place was, so I kept quiet. The rest of the family entered with long, somber faces. We were guided down a hall away from the main chapel and into the curtained off area set just for us. My grandmother cried softly but made little noise. My parents were quiet and solemn. My brother looked very out of place.

Before the service began, we were given an opportunity to view Grandpa's body. My step-grandmother and the rest of the family went first. After they were seated, we were led to view Grandpa. I stood beside my mother and looked in the coffin. A thing resembling Grandpa lay there in a suit and tie. To me it appeared empty. Grandpa wasn't there. Mother instructed me to touch his body. I did so while not knowing what to expect. His skin was cold to the touch and reminded me of a chicken before it was cooked. It also confirmed, in my mind, that Grandpa no longer dwelt within the container in front of me. We returned to our space and sat. Others lined up to view the body after we left.

I just couldn't get into the sadness of it all. I felt a joy permeate my entire being. I could hardly sit still for the happiness surrounding me. And then I heard singing. At first I thought it came from the funeral service which had already begun. The music they were playing came from traditional Christian hymns. The music I heard rang from the rafters with joy and celebration. I was sure a party was taking place, only I couldn't see it. There was so much happiness. If I had any doubts about angelic choirs, they disappeared that day. I had difficulty following the earthly service, being caught up in the Heavenly one going on around me. Grandpa was having a fabulous time.

I did ignore the Heavenly choir for a little bit when the minister gave the eulogy. I heard him announce that Grandpa had worked for a rival company, instead of the correct one. Grandpa and Dad both worked for the Spokane, Portland, & Seattle Railroad, more commonly known as the SP & S. The rival company was the Southern Pacific Railroad, with the initials SP. Several people gasped as many of Grandpa's office colleagues attended the service.

The Heavenly party thought it very funny. Hilarity spread all over the chapel including our curtained nook. No one seemed to notice. I couldn't figure out why people were so sad and so many were crying. Some expressed anger. The minister's small mistake became the most talked about part of the entire service. Some were sure Grandpa would have rolled over in his coffin, if it were possible. Grandpa thought it was funny.

I later told my mother about my experience. We talked about it at length. She was fascinated. For some reason, I never felt comfortable about sharing that experience, although I did tell my boyfriend, who was also intrigued. We both agreed it was best not to say anything about it to anyone else. Such things were not discussed in the '60s. Anyone with an experience like mine was often termed queer. (At that time, the word *queer* was used as an adjective not a noun. We lived in a sheltered community and had no knowledge of the gay community.)

After this experience, I questioned all the religious teachings concerning death. Nothing fit. Why were we here? became the number one question for many years to come. I began to doubt everything I had learned up to this point. I decided that God could not be an angry and vengeful god, if parties of great joy occurred whenever someone died.

Then the question arose: What about serial killers and Hitler? Did they have joyful transitions? I hoped not.

4

Another Unusual Experience

*Death—especially when unexpected—has a way of wiping
away the filters we've put on our lives and giving us
a new perspective about where we are
and where we may be headed.*

A. C. ASEH

A year and a half later I married my high school sweetheart. We spent a two-week honeymoon in Hawaii and came home to Oregon State University where we both were engineering students. He was two years ahead of me.

I adored my husband's family. Being invited to their house was a special treat and I looked forward to each occasion. Dinner was always a fun time. My father-in-law loved to make puns. I never knew what he was going to say next. This was new to me. While my father was a great story teller, I don't think I ever heard anyone play with puns until I met this delightful man.

I had a special relationship with my father-in-law. We loved to play word games with each other. He was a worthy opponent and won most of the games. I learned a lot about the English language and the use of words from him.

Four weeks to the day after our marriage, my husband sat up in bed at two o'clock in the morning and began to cry. I asked him what was the matter and he replied he was crying because he loved his father. I held him for a long time. When the tears stopped flowing we talked about how he felt and why. He had no answers. By six o'clock that morning we were on our way home.

Our arrival came as a bit of a pleasant surprise. My father-in-law was leading a Mazama climb, with members of our church as part of the group, on a climb up Mount Adams. Our minister was part of the party. Most of the climbers were teenagers.

Near the summit, they encountered an unexpected blizzard that caused a complete white out. No one could see more than a couple of feet ahead. Two boys panicked and ran. My father-in-law asked everyone to rope together so no one would get lost. That is when he discovered the two boys were missing. He was a very caring man who took his responsibilities seriously. The loss of the two boys weighed heavily on his shoulders.

Fortunately, he knew the mountain well. He managed to guide the group to a point where stakes could be seen for guiding climbers through an area thick with dangerous crevasses. Our minister noticed my father-in-law was having trouble breathing. It was also getting dark. They set up camp and everyone crowded into a tent. Our minister had the young people lay on both sides of my father-in-law to keep him warm. At two o'clock in the morning our minister pulled the children away as my father-in-law had passed away.

Our first confirmation that something was amiss came with a phone call from our minister. He said he was coming over to see us. He made no mention of my father-in-law. Our anxiety increased. Two of my husband's sisters were at home. One lived out of town and we had to call her later. We waited anxiously until the minister got there. My mother-in-law wanted to feed us. It was late in the afternoon. No one wanted to eat. We all knew the news was not good. At six o'clock our minister finally arrived. He took my mother-in-law aside and told her about my father-in-law's passing. A few minutes later the rest of us heard the story. My father-in-law died of hypothermia.

His death led to some serious studies on how stress can bring on hypothermia.

The two boys managed to find a ridge and made their way safely down the mountain. They were found later that day.

Now I had more questions. How did my husband know something serious had happened to his father? Why did we feel the need to rush home? How did this fit in with my ultimate quest?

5

My Stepfather's Transition

I'm very thankful for our house, our cars, and all of the blessings I have in my life, but I try to always remember that they won't fit in my casket when it's time for me to go.

Gobel Brockman

My stepfather was a very superstitious person. He was certain he was going to die, because the doctors at the Mayo Clinic insisted on doing open heart surgery on Friday the 13th. He begged them to perform the surgery on another day, but their schedules didn't allow it. There were complications, and he never was quite the same afterwards.

He suffered from congestive heart failure for the next two years. When he stopped eating and drinking we knew the end was near. Hospice was called in. It took two weeks for my stepfather to make his transition.

His personality changed when he quit taking nourishment and fluids. I perceived him as a very confident man. He and his business partner ran a successful truck wholesale company. He was assertive, knew what he wanted, and how to get it.

I didn't know how prejudiced he was until my mother became concerned because some of the hospice nurses and caregivers were of other races. Mother was sure they would not be accepted by my stepfather. It turned out she needn't have worried. He accepted everyone. He often expressed gratitude to everyone who helped him.

My strong, dominant, assertive stepfather had turned into a very kind and gentle man. I thought his personality had left and the true spirit of who he was had surfaced. As I sat by his side for hours on end, I pondered on these things.

Was this personality the real one? Was the one I had always known something he had adopted for this lifetime?

My mother and I rarely got more than a couple hours sleep each night. My stepfather had sundowner's syndrome. He slept off and on during the day and was awake most of the night. He also had a form of sleep apnea. I am not sure if that is the correct terminology, but it is what one of the hospice people called it. He would be awake and then suddenly fall asleep. While asleep his breath came in and out with a noise not unlike coma breathing. It is louder than normal breathing. Each breath is deep and sounds like it comes from the back of the throat.

My step-father started greeting people we couldn't see. He would be talking to someone and before he could tell us who it was, he would lapse into the apnea breath. When he woke again he wouldn't remember who it was he greeted.

One day he called out, "Hi. It's been a long time since I saw you last." He had a big grin on his face and it was obvious he was delighted to see whoever it was. Of course, he went to sleep again and never could tell us who it was.

Twelve days after all this began, he lapsed into the coma breathing and never came out of it. I felt his spirit had left his body. I can't say why I felt that way. It just seemed to me he wasn't there. I had had similar feelings whenever I viewed a body during a funeral. The person was gone. Other than the heart problems, my step father had been in great physical condition. He liked to play tennis before he got ill. As a result, it took a long time for his system to shut down. I think he got tired of waiting and simply left. After two days of being in a coma his body finally stopped working.

It was quite peaceful during those two days we waited for his body to stop working. I got bored sitting vigil over his body. Nothing was happening. I no longer sensed other beings around the bed. Up until then, I could sense the room was full of beings I could not see. It was different from when my grandfather passed. His was a joyful occasion. This was a happy occasion, too. But different. I heard no singing or laughter. I felt like the beings who were present were patiently waiting for him to leave his body and then they would escort him home.

By this time, I had no doubt there was life after death. My grandfather's passing confirmed that for me. My father-in-law communicated with my husband. Of that I had no doubt either, even though no words were spoken. That my step-father communicated with people who had crossed the veil before him, seemed very real to my mother and me. Why I knew he left his body before it ceased to function did bother me a lot. How did I know? I didn't see it leave. Why are we here? still went unanswered. I felt like I was getting close to the answers somehow.

6

My Dad

*I am not afraid of dying.
It's the process of getting there that worries me.*

DON THOMAS

I had good parents. They had their weaknesses just like anybody else and they made some mistakes while raising my brother and me. However, we had little or no knowledge of incest, bigotry, or racial hatred. It was a time of innocence. I adored my dad. We had some differences of opinion from time to time, but that didn't change my opinion of him.

I grew up in a world of reason and logic. My dad was a civil engineer as was my grandpa. They both designed railroad bridges. One of Dad's bridges even got written up in a couple of magazines. My mother's father was a lawyer. Events like what happened at Grandpa's funeral just didn't happen, which is a major reason why I kept quiet about my experience.

In 1997, a friend of mine introduced me to Healing Touch Program™. I loved the first class so much, I took every class they taught and eventually became a certified instructor. My experiences as a biofield therapist, also called an energy medicine practitioner among other things, opened many doors for me. I found myself looking inside for answers. I found guides willing to help whenever I asked. I began to notice things that were beyond my understanding, yet were just as real as the book in your hand.

In the spring of 2004, I became concerned. I had invited my dad and my stepmother to Easter dinner. He said he felt too tired and could we do it another time. My alarm bells went off, and I decided to go pay them an unexpected visit. I took an Easter lily with me as an excuse for dropping in.

My stepmother answered the door and said my father was resting in his den. I gave her the plant and she invited me in. I walked into Dad's den and immediately knew something was very wrong with him. I have never been very good at seeing auras, but I could sense something was not right with my dad. My gut feeling was that my father was about to die. Until then Dad had always been a healthy man. He rarely caught so much as a cold. He loved to play golf. In earlier years, he skied so well he won a few trophies. Due to an unfortunate accident that rendered him unable to ski as well as he liked to do, he quit the sport.

Dad's hands were shaking. I found out he hadn't been able to play golf in the last few weeks. Dad talked about a dental problem and thought that was the cause. He had been given Novocain for some dental work. Before it wore off, he accidentally bit his lip. The resulting sore didn't heal. He went back to the dentist, who gave him some antibiotics. The sore still didn't heal.

I had a good old-fashioned hissy fit and insisted he go see a doctor the next day. If he didn't go, I would come get him and take him to one. Reluctantly they agreed Dad would see a doctor.

Bless my stepmother. She was as concerned as I was. She got Dad to see his doctor the next day. She called me while on the way to the hospital after his appointment. I dropped what I was doing and raced to meet them.

When I got there, the doctor took me aside and asked if Dad had been exposed to any chemicals during his lifetime. I told him Dad had been exposed to DDT (dichlorodiphenyltrichloroethane) while working as a roadmaster for the railroad. He had also been exposed to a chemical similar to agent orange while checking tracks after his company merged with others. He personally walked or rode over two thousand miles of track looking for weaknesses and the need for repairs. Both DDT and agent orange were used as herbicides to keep the tracks clear of weeds.

The doctor sighed. My dad had acute myelocytic leukemia, which is different from myeloid leukemia. Someone mentioned the myelocytic form of leukemia occurs more commonly in children. In adults, it usually meant the patient had been exposed to hazardous chemicals. This form of leukemia grows very rapidly. He gave my dad a few weeks to live at best. His case was so advanced, treatment might buy him a couple of months, but he would be suffering from the effects of chemotherapy the whole time.

I learned things about my father I didn't know through this experience. Dad stayed in the hospital for a couple of days while they completed the testing of his condition. My father loved to smoke. It was one of his most cherished delights in life. He had to wear a patch while in the hospital, as smoking was not allowed. He took that in stride, with a minimum of grumbling.

Even today, I laugh about comments that came up several times concerning the smoking thing. Dad was tickled pink his disease was not brought on by smoking. It probably didn't help the process, but it wasn't the cause. He even exhibited a sense of pride over this. I was worried at first, because I am allergic to cigarette smoke and I knew I would be exposed to the smoke all the time I was with Dad. I shouldn't have worried. For the duration of Dad's remaining time, I even lit his cigarettes for him, and had no adverse allergy symptoms. Interesting how the mind works and controls our bodies.

Dad did not want any form of chemotherapy. They sent him home once the tests were completed and all of them confirmed the doctor's original diagnosis. It turns out Dad was a great believer in dying with dignity. He belonged to the Hemlock Society, which is not quite a legal organization in Oregon. We quickly found out they no longer were functioning.

Dad wanted to go the self-assisted death with dignity route. Neither my stepmother nor I were prepared for that. It upset her greatly. She argued with Dad endlessly. She felt there should be other options and wanted to explore them, perhaps even going for a second opinion.

Dad knew he was dying. He didn't know how long it would take and wanted to speed things along. In my heart, I knew Dad would not have to take that final drink. This made it easier for me to go along with him. I can't say why I knew this with certainty. I just knew.

We contacted family after Dad came home from the

hospital. My brother got leave and flew home. He could stay only a few days because he was a college professor and felt an obligation to his students. It was very difficult for him to leave Dad, and has since regretted it, as he would have liked to have stayed and then later attend the memorial service.

My aunt and uncle wanted to fly out the following week. I called my aunt back and told her she needed to come now, as I didn't think Dad was going to be around that long. She heard me. They flew out the next morning.

It was difficult for me during this time. My intuition was so strong. I just knew Dad wasn't going to be with us for much longer, maybe another week at best. I had nothing to go on except that gut feeling. Coaxing people to come quickly without a valid reason wasn't easy. Yet they came anyway. Perhaps some part of their inner knowing told them his time was short and my sense of urgency confirmed it for them.

Dad was put on hospice. They contacted the state about Dad wanting to go the route of assisted suicide. The hospice people were wonderful. They set everything up for Dad including oxygen. We had to turn the oxygen off every time Dad smoked a cigarette. It became a point of humor, which helped everyone. His last days were as comfortable as can be in such a situation.

The state people came out and interviewed Dad. Their main concern was to prove that he was in his right mind and logical in his decision. Dad was very firm about it. One of the questions they asked him was to which political party he belonged. To my surprise, he answered Democrat. He said he had been a Republican most of his life and that he didn't like the way the party was going. He didn't like the Democrats either, but he thought they were a better choice. The Republican party had become a disappointment to him.

Dad's sense of humor showed up during the interview. I heard him say that he wasn't afraid of death. It was the process of getting there that bothered him. Everybody laughed. I think that is true for a lot of us. Me, too.

When it came time to decide who would help Dad drink that last drink, there was some consternation. My stepmother couldn't do it. It had to be a close relative. My brother wasn't present at this time. That left me. I agreed to be the one to help him. I was acutely uncomfortable about that decision. My job was to help people heal, not to help them die. I didn't know that death is sometimes the cure.

We had to wait three weeks after the approval came through. I breathed a sigh of relief, because I knew it wasn't needed as Dad wouldn't be with us that long. I was right. Dad died twelve days after his initial diagnosis.

The day before he died, I had my hands on both sides of his chest. Energy flowed freely. I relaxed and let it happen.

Then a strange thing happened. Dad turned to me and said, "That feels so good."

Dad once told me he respected my work as a biofield therapist/energy medicine practitioner, but had no understanding of it. I think it scared him. I once demonstrated for him the use of a pendulum for the assessment of chakras. When Dad tried it, the pendulum never moved.

Energy work does not require reason and logic in order to function. That afternoon, Dad suddenly had an understanding of what I was doing. It was a poignant moment in our relationship.

Dad made his transition quietly. He passed into a coma late in the morning and stayed in the coma for four and a half hours. My stepmother and my aunt and I kept vigil at his bedside. Through our tears during that whole time, I felt the power of women and how we can come together in the most difficult of circumstances. My uncle waited in their hotel room. It hurt him too much to be there in the last moments.

As Dad took his last breath, he came out of the coma. A look of pure joy came over his face. I thought maybe he was recognizing loved ones and seemed delighted to see them. I am not sure what it was he saw. The look of joy stayed on the face of his body long after he left it.

I learned a lot more about my father at the time of his

memorial service. It took place at the country club connected to his favorite golf course. Over two hundred people came. It was standing room only and some had to observe from outside of the room, looking through open windows and doors.

Quite a few people spoke. Most of the stories had to do with things my dad had done for them. I felt very proud of him that day. Many of the stories were humorous. I told a few stories myself. He was a good man.

After Dad died, to my surprise he showed up whenever I did healing work with clients. His presence was so strong even people who had never encountered spirits of any kind asked who the man was in the room. Dad wanted to know about what it was that I was doing. This continued for three or four months. One day he didn't show up. He didn't say good-bye or anything. I asked my guides about it and was told he had moved on. Once in a while I sense his essence and think he might be checking up on me. I don't know for sure.

Many years have passed since those first two transitions. Actually, several family members had made transitions in between my father-in-law's transition and my dad's. They were uneventful. I was disappointed each time, as I had come to expect something miraculous to happen at each one. When it didn't, I wondered why.

My search for the answer to the question of why am I here, why is everybody here, was yet unanswered.

7

The Continued Search

The path to our destination is not always a straight one.
We go down the wrong road, we get lost, we turn back.
Maybe it doesn't matter which road we embark on.
Maybe what matters is that we embark.

BARBARA HALL

By the time of Dad's transition, I had studied Buddhism, Catholicism, Zen, and several protestant religions. I came into the Catholic Church due to a second marriage. My husband was what is called a cradle Catholic, meaning he was born into the church. When I joined the Catholic Church, we lived in a Jesuit community. It was a perfect way for me to come into the church since Jesuits practice mediation and hands-on healing. The priests were wonderful. I had studied Zen for five years before I married my second husband. They liked my devotion to meditation and my beliefs in right thinking and right way of life. But they didn't know the answer as to why we are here.

I had read everything I could find on the teachings of Buddha. At the time, if someone demanded I give them a name to my faith I would have said I am a Christian Buddhist or maybe a Catholic Buddhist. However, none of it fit. Even as a practicing Catholic, I knew it wasn't the right label for me. I did feel I was a part of a community as a Catholic, more than at any other time in my exploration of religions. I was deeply disappointed neither Catholicism nor Buddhism answered the quest question.

Buddhism came close. Buddhists do not believe in a supreme being the way Christians do. I have read several sources stating that Buddha did not acknowledge a supreme being. Many followers of Buddhism have a god they worship in addition to the Buddha teachings. I think it's more of a philosophy than a religion.

I read somewhere that there has never been a war fought between the different Buddhist sects over which one is the correct one. I hope that is true. Christianity could learn from that.

New questions arose. What determined the difference between good and evil? Who decided which was which?

One of my favorite blessings came from two good friends who introduced me to the Living Enrichment Center. The first time I attended, I cried through most of the service. I felt I had come home to something I had been searching for all of my life. Again, the concept of being responsible for my own life came up. This time I was listening with both ears.

Mary Manin Morressey was the lead minister. She is a great story teller and often uses her own life experiences to emphasize a point, much to the consternation of her family. When I first attended the church, I was living in Boise, Idaho. The church was located in Beaverton, Oregon some three hundred and forty miles away. It was a long commute and I didn't get there nearly as often as I would have liked.

During one service Alan Cohen addressed the congregation. He spoke to my heart. I heard him repeat a sentence from *A Course in Miracles*. It is as true for me today as it was then. "The presence of fear is a sure sign you are relying on your own strength." Wow. I loved it. I had to know more. The day before I left to go home, I knew I had to buy that book. I managed to find the twenty-five dollars to pay for it. Money was scarce for me at the time.

I went to the church bookstore, only to find it was closed. I sat down by the door and waited for it to open thinking the store sales force had gone out to lunch. I sat there for almost an hour. Finally, a kind man saw me there and asked why I was sitting near the door. I told him I wanted to buy the book. He told me the bookstore was closed on Monday's. My heart sank. I had to go home to Boise the next day.

"I happen to have a key to the bookstore," he said. "I'll open it for you and sell you the book." Someone was looking out for me. I was unaware of guardian angels and guides at that point, but I knew someone or something was helping me with my quests. It also confirmed my growing belief that we create our own worlds. The concept of whether or not angels or guides or unseen helpers or whatever you want to call them, actually help us create our worlds hadn't yet occurred to me.

A Course in Miracles is not an easy book to read. I decided to do the workbook section. I felt I would learn more by doing than by reading. I knew of no one in Boise who could answer my questions though. I sent Alan Cohen a letter via the Living Enrichment Center. Someone there very kindly forwarded the letter to him. (Again, this was before the Internet.) He answered it. I did the workbook thing for the entire year it recommended. As busy a person as he is, Alan answered every letter and every question. We both shared a lot of humor during the process. I am most grateful to him. I hope I can be as gracious.

The Continued Search

During that year, I got back into the practice of meditating. I learned a lot about forgiveness. I still did not get an answer as to why we are here. Not even a hint, at least that I noticed.

Shortly after I completed the year I moved back home to Oregon. I attended the Living Enrichment Center on a regular basis. The church moved to a new location in Wilsonville, Oregon. I hated to miss a single Sunday. I volunteered a lot. I read hundreds of books. My library at home grew as I acquired book after book that might have a clue as to the answer to my quest.

And one arose. Sometime during those years, I came across a new concept: planet Earth is a school. People line up to be born here. They create contracts before they come in. Once the contracts are fulfilled, people make their transition back home. There they study what they had done with their lives and decide on either further study in their next life or to try something new. That was an eye-opener. It felt sort of right. I worked with it for many years to come. It answered many "why" questions. But not all of them.

Still, I bought it hook, line and sinker while watching a movie years later. The movie featured a story about African Americans fighting for the South during the Civil War. Just before a battle, a bunch of them were discussing why they were willing to do this. It wasn't what they said that got me. I realized each one was there for his own reason even though he was not conscious of it. Some wanted to know what it was like to be brave. Others wanted to experience cowardice. Many were shot and either killed or wounded—learning opportunities both.

It dawned on me that we will always have wars because they provide a terrific learning ground for all kinds of experiences. If Earth were indeed a school for souls to learn about themselves, then wars made sense. In a sense wars are shortcuts to many learning experiences. The concept felt right, but it was not one I was willing to discuss unless I felt safe with similar-minded people. This was way out of bounds for me. Besides, I still questioned the concept. I felt like I wasn't getting the whole picture.

It wasn't long after this, I had a talk with Lucifer about good and evil. I had formed a communicative relationship with my unseen helpers and I asked one of them about the difference between good and evil. Mary had given a sermon about how nothing was either good or bad, right or wrong, until someone labeled it as such. This was new territory and I wanted to explore it.

My favorite guide suggested I talk to Lucifer, as he was the foremost authority on the subject. I envisioned myself standing on a hilltop and called down Lucifer. Even though

I had heard him called the Devil, Satan, and the prince of evil, I felt no fear. I knew my guides were there to protect me, because I asked them to. I felt their presence quite strongly, although they made no move to interfere.

When Lucifer appeared in front of me I asked him, "What is the difference between good and evil? How will I know the difference?"

He produced a yardstick and held it where I could easily see it. "This end," he said, pointing to the lower numbers, "Is the good end."

He moved a hand to the other end of the yardstick, "And this is the evil end."

He then moved a hand to the middle. "Here is a large middle ground, so where does good leave off and evil begin?"

I couldn't answer that question, the way he put it.

He continued even though I didn't say anything out loud. "I can see you don't know. We decided this side is evil, yes?"

I nodded.

"And this side is good, yes?"

Again, I nodded.

"But it is the same stick. How can one end be different from the other when it is all one piece of wood?"

"Because you said it was," I said, not sure of myself,

but knowing he wanted me to say something.

"Exactly," he said. "Because I said it was. But is it really?

I waited for him to go on.

"A thing or event is neither good nor evil until you decided that is what it is."

"What about Hitler?" (Hitler was my favorite villain of the day. I had read a lot of books about the holocaust.)

"What about him?" said Lucifer.

"Well," I said, "He caused a lot of people to be killed. He wasn't a very nice man."

"How do you know? Have you met him?"

"Well, no," I said. "I have read a lot about him. The killing of the Jews and all those other people seems to me to be an evil thing."

"Your call. He thought he was doing something to help his people. To him it was a solution to a difficult problem. He thought he was doing something good."

"I can't agree with that," I replied.

"Of course, you can't. It's your perspective. That doesn't make it right or wrong, good or bad. Merely a different point of view from his."

I had to admit he had me there. I didn't like it though. It seemed to me it was giving Hitler free reign to do all the destruction he wanted to do.

As if reading my mind again, Lucifer said, "Exactly so. He was free to do as he wished. It is called free will."

"How about all those people he had killed? Did they have free will?"

"Yes," he answered.

"How can you call it free will? What choice did they have as to whether they lived or died? Hitler took that away from them."

"Did he?" said Lucifer, "Did he really? They all agreed to participate in that experience before they came to this planet. Those that changed their minds left Germany before the atrocities began."

Years passed before I could fully understand what he was trying to tell me.

In the meantime, I had many discussions with my unseen helpers about free will. As I understand it, planet Earth has been designated a place where free will reigns as a supreme law. Beings from other worlds, universes, and dimensions are not allowed to interfere in any way with our lives except when asked or given permission. Even the guides cannot help unless they are asked. We can do anything we want to each other. The interaction is what makes this place so interesting.

Now this became a problem for me. Asking for help, especially from someone I couldn't see, was not part of my daily existence. I grew up in a family where we were all expected to walk in strength. Crying was punishable. Showing emotion in public wasn't done. Weakness was frowned upon. This caused my brother and me a lot of grief. We had the choice to not buy into that. We just didn't know it.

Several years ago, I had an office and was practicing Healing Touch. In the early years, I came to recognize a helper. He came for every healing. He never steered me wrong. Because I was unsure of myself and wanting to help my clients, I overcame this fear of asking for help. The only time something didn't go well, was when I misinterpreted his advice. I always ask for it before I do any healing work.

For a long time, I wanted to know where I could have done better. It wasn't easy to do work that I couldn't see, that I could only feel. Early on I made the decision not to trust what I saw in the energy field. It was too easy to make up a reason for whatever showed up, a trick of the light, hopeful imagination, etc. I had trouble making up stuff about what I felt with my hands. I eventually learned to trust what I felt. To confirm those impressions, I asked my guide for explanations. It became a practice on the way home each day for him to critique how I did. He became one of my dearest friends and still is today.

Many of the critiques involved my ego. Some days it

took quite a beating. I had to learn to trust that my hands were going to the right place instead of where I thought they should go. Often it seemed quite bizarre. Why put my hands on someone's big toe, when the problem was a pain somewhere else, above the waist. (Biofield therapists often look for cause rather than just alleviate symptoms.) My guides were always right. I stopped questioning eventually, but I still like validations.

A client came to see me. He had been exploring the different dimensions and realms of our world. His helpers felt alien to me and I was careful when I worked on him. My guides warned me not to become too involved as he was going down a path that wasn't meant for me.

At the same time, I belonged to a women's study group in a nearby city. We met every month. We have studied many books over the years. We get into some lively discussions. It was, and still is, loads of fun.

This man's sister was part of the group at that time. As we were leaving a meeting, she told me her brother sent his good wishes to me. I told her to tell him thank you. At that moment, I knew I had done something wrong, but I didn't know what it was.

A friend of mine carpooled with me to the meetings. It was my turn to drive. She had been studying shamanism with Alberto Villoldo for many years. We were chatting about the meeting and I told her about how I felt I had done something wrong. Her thought was I should be careful around the client and even suggested I quit seeing him.

At some point, I became aware I had a truck in front of me, one behind, and one to the left of me. I was completely hemmed in. Before I could react to that, I felt a pressure on the front of my neck. It felt like someone had their hands around my neck and was trying to strangle me. At first it was just an odd sensation, and I wasn't frightened. The pressure increased and I became aware something needed to be done. Much more pressure and I wouldn't be able to breathe.

My friend was in the middle of telling me a story. I remember reaching over and grabbing her hand. I managed to convey that I was in trouble. She looked at me and saw something was happening for real. It wasn't just my imagination.

She thought for a moment and then asked, "Do you have any water with you?"

"Yes," I croaked. "It's in my knitting bag."

She rummaged around in the knitting bag that was behind my seat and found the bottle. Then she searched her purse and brought out a bottle of special water used for shamanic purposes. It smelled like cheap perfume. She poured a few drops into my water bottle and then filled her mouth with some of the contents. I still laugh at what happened next. She spat it out all over me.

"Demon, be gone!" she commanded. It left just as quickly as it came in. We broke into giggles. I don't know if it was the laughter that chased away the demon, or being showered with the holy water she spat on me, or both. It worked.

The truck on the left disappeared. I don't know if it fell behind or sped ahead. My safe little cocoon opened up and I was free to pass the truck in front of me.

We have discussed that incident many times through the years. We both laugh about it. I feel we learned an important lesson. In saying the words *thank you*, I had invited in one of the entities that traveled with my client. I labeled it a demon, knowing full well it was my label, and had no reference as to whether the thing was good or evil. I have kept that label. The words, thank you, acknowledged the entity's existence and opened the door for it to interfere with my world.

Demons are always looking for ways to get permission to work with humans. Saying thank you is a way of acknowledging the existence of a spiritual being and they take that as an invitation. There are many others. Demons are very sneaky about it. They use phrases like "thank you" as a way to justify their coming in and causing havoc. I asked the guides about it, because it seemed to me this was interfering with my free will.

My head guide said, "Because you agreed to the idea that 'thank you' was an invitation to the demon to do its thing, it was able to do what it wanted."

"Huh?"

"It's like your conversation with Lucifer," my guide said, when he saw that I was confused. "You labeled it. Thank you usually is an expression of gratitude. You gave it another meaning."

"I did, didn't I?" I said.

"Yes," he replied. "You must guard your thoughts at all times. Too often you say one thing and intend for it to mean something else. Looking back, you recognize your mistake and make up something to cover it."

"Do you mean, if I had said something other than thank you, it wouldn't have happened?"

"Oh, I think it would have happened anyway. This way you can blame yourself more easily. The demon would have had to have been sneakier in the way it came in. And did it ever occur to you, we might have had a hand in your experience by sealing you off and protecting you through the use of those three trucks?"

"The trucks occurred to me. Were you the demon?"

"No, I don't do that kind of thing. When it came at you, I created some protection while it conversed with you. I didn't know, at first, that it was going to try to choke you."

For years, I tried to toss the whole thing off as my imagination. However, my friend had felt the presence of the thing and is not quite sure what she saw near my throat. She knows she saw something. With her confirmation of the experience, it has been hard to say it was imaginary.

8

My Own Near-Death Experience

The value of that one near miss with death has been a positive, a reawakening to the value of each day. Each one of us has only a limited time on this earth; no one can predict when your time will end.

BYRON PULSIFER

As I write these stories, I can feel the emotions of the transition experiences mentioned earlier. It is as if they happened yesterday. None of them prepared me for my next experience.

Before Dad's death, I began having dental problems myself. One day I bit into something and one of my back molars broke. I didn't think much about it. I thought I had bit into something hard, even though I couldn't find anything hard in my mouth. I didn't have two cents to my name and no dental insurance. I let it go. The tooth began to crumble over time. It didn't hurt and I had other things on my mind, so I ignored it.

A couple of years passed and other teeth began to break. I put it off as something to do with menopause. Money grew increasingly tight at the time. My teeth were not that important on my list of things to do. Dad's death, problems with an ex-spouse, and a move crowded my thoughts. I also was developing a healing practice. I was about to learn we are not meant to heal alone.

One day I bent over to feed the dog and felt a wave of dizziness come over me. I made it to the bedroom and laid down. It was awful. I cannot put it any stronger. I decided that I had better see a doctor.

He could find no reason for the vertigo. He even sent me to the hospital for an MRI. It showed fluid behind the ear, but no tumor and none of the usual causes of vertigo. That doctor told me antibiotics wouldn't help. He sent me home and told me to live with it. Living with it was not on my to-do list.

I had four episodes where the vertigo was so severe I had to go to an emergency room. They would give me shots for the nausea and a five-day prescription for antibiotics. I would feel better for a few days, but the vertigo always returned.

Vertigo never left me. For a full year, I lived with the world whirling around me. The doctors prescribed Meclizine, a newer version of Dramamine, for nausea. People take it for sea sickness and other causes of vertigo and nausea. A friend suggested I get some C-bands. They are knitted bracelets with a round button sewn on the inside. The button goes over a pressure point along a meridian line located on the inside of the wrist. It helped a little and I wore them night and day.

I talked with a good friend who had had a similar experience. Her vertigo came from an infection in her teeth. My alarm bells went off. Here I was with teeth breaking down. Perhaps it wasn't something to do with menopause. Could it be I had an infection in my teeth?

I went to see another ear-nose-throat doctor. I begged him for antibiotics. He refused to give them to me. He told me to lay off the salt. He said that Americans ate too much salt and that I should lay off packaged foods as they were a big source of sodium. I told him I had a vegetable garden and grew a lot of my own food. I rarely add salt to anything. He didn't believe me and sent me home.

I had another bad vertigo session and ended up in the emergency room again. They gave me another five-day prescription for antibiotics. They also told me to see a dentist. I gave in and went to the dentist.

A wisdom tooth, a late bloomer, came in about a year

before all this started. It was porous and brought in bacteria. The bugs spread throughout all of my jaw, top and bottom. I had to have six teeth removed immediately. I lost two more a short time later.

My oral surgeon is a delight. The rooms are pleasant and comfortable. No instruments of destruction show in her operating rooms. They are all brought in on a portable table behind the patient. She worked with me. I didn't want a lot of drugs. I am allergic to many of the usual pain and anti-anxiety medicines.

I put myself in a meditative trance. When I started to come out of it, she could tell by my blood pressure. She'd suggest I go back into the trance and then continue pulling out teeth. This worked very well for both us. Her tray contained ten syringes of pain medication at the beginning of the session. Nine remained when we finished.

I was sent home with a pint of strawberry Häagen-Dazs ice cream, some synthetic codeine, and no antibiotics. My daughter stayed with me the first two days of recovery. She talked me into taking a codeine pill. I knew I was allergic to codeine. Because this was synthetic codeine, my doctor thought I could handle it. I decided I would try half a pill. When the ropes started coming down from the ceiling, I knew even synthetic codeine was not for me. My daughter went home the next day. She took the pills with her in case someone in her family had a need for them.

The next morning, I woke up with what felt like a stitch in my side. It was quite painful. I was still experiencing vertigo, and my jaws hurt where the teeth had been removed. I managed to feed the dog and collapsed in a recliner chair located in what I call my work room. The pain in my side intensified from all the effort.

An angel appeared in front of me. It told me I had a blood clot in my lung, and that it was time for me to go home. The next moment I will never forget. One moment I had all the worries and cares of a normal human being. The next moment I had none. I felt totally free.

I do mean free. I had no worries of any kind. I felt like the weight of the world had been lifted from my shoulders. It was wonderful to feel free of all earthly concerns. I mentioned my dog and was told he would be well taken care of. I knew my children no longer needed me. They had developed good lives of their own. I was free, totally free.

It was an exhilarating experience. I loved it. The world was so beautiful. I felt surrounded with love. It reminded me of a baby cradled in the arms of an adoring mother. I was the baby. I basked in the joy of the moment. I was ready to go.

At some point one of my guardian angels spoke up. He talked about my having had a difficult life. It would be nice for me to have a few years of fun. I thought about this for a bit. I was still in a state of euphoria. I very much wanted to go to the other side. I also wanted to know what fun was waiting for me in this life. I knew that I would eventually get to go home, so why not experience this time of earthly pleasures? Being in a place of no worries made it so easy. I didn't really care either way. My guardian angel pushed for me to stay. Either way was fine with me, so I stayed here.

I have not regretted that decision. Not every moment of my present life is what I would call fun. When I feel like I have been short-changed on the fun thing, I have to step back and look at the world from a different point of view. A good book is fraught with hazards, problems and all kinds of mayhem. A Pollyanna book is boring after the first couple of pages. I have learned that even when I am in my stuff and fussing over this and that, I am still enjoying myself. I don't always admit that, however. When I can step back and look at things from a different point of view, I like to ponder on how things will turn out. It all comes down to my choices.

It never occurred to me during that experience to ask my favorite question—Why are we here?

9

A Student Makes His Transition

*It is well to give when asked, but it is better
to give unasked, through understanding.*

KAHLIL GIBRAN

A couple of years later, one of my students was admitted to a local Veterans Administration Hospital. He was dying of cancer and wanted to see me. I didn't know he was seriously ill until I got his phone call. I hurried up to the hospital. We talked for a bit. I did Healing Touch on him. I wanted to talk to him about the other side of the veil and what would happen when he made his transition, but felt shy about it. I went home without saying anything. Oreg, my lead healing guide, bawled me out for my shyness all the way home from the hospital, which is an hour's drive when traffic is light. Ahem.

Transition was a subject I began to feel I knew well, but my answers differed from most folks I knew. I had my own experiences, plus others, that told me this was a time of great joy. Celebration of a life well lived is a common event that goes unnoticed by most people.

So, what is a life well lived? In my not-so-humble opinion, no one can answer that except for themselves.

Near-death experiences offer a glimpse of the beginnings of the process of crossing over. Because no one that I know of has ever gone beyond a certain point, I cannot say what is for sure on the other side. I have noticed that people find what they expect when they begin the experience. Some are met by friends and family who passed over ahead of them. Guides and guardian angels greet others. I know of a few who thought they were met by Jesus. In my course of studies, many writers have stated that a person's expectations govern who greets them, and how quickly they integrate themselves into the afterlife.

"Truth is truth," my guide said. "It is time you spoke it."

I went back the next day.

My friend wanted to know what was going to happen to him and started asking questions. I told him of my near-death experience. My studies and experiences had taken me far afield of my Christian upbringing. I got brave and told him what I knew to be true. At one point, I noticed other patients had gathered at the door to listen to our conversation. I saw a couple of them nod in agreement at something I said. That gave me courage to continue.

I told him all about the angel that appeared in front of me. I went into great detail about how I felt so free of all concerns, responsibilities, and all the things I thought I had to do. I even told him things I had forgotten. I couldn't describe the angel. I had felt its presence rather than saw it clearly. The guardian angel behind me was just a voice, a comfortable voice that seemed familiar

It didn't seem to bother my friend that I felt rather than saw the angel. I saw him nod in agreement when I talked about the absolute joy of being free of all earthly concerns. I could visualize it quite clearly in my mind even though a couple of years had passed. It's just as clear today.

I went back the next day. My friend had made his transition during the night. The nurse told me it was a very peaceful one

After I left, she said he relaxed and let his body do its thing. He had no pain, or at least never mentioned any. I had done pain relieving techniques during each of my previous visits. I don't know if that was why he was no longer in pain. My ego would like to think so.

It can be quite uncomfortable and even frightening to the spirit when the heart stops. I believe he relaxed and found his way out of his body before it stopped functioning. I think he had no fear of his passing

10

A Client's Transition

The soul would have no rainbow if the eyes had no tears.
NATIVE AMERICAN PROVERB

I have had marvelous teachers my whole life. They still show up from time to time. I love it. This one came quite unexpectedly.

I got a call from a Healing Touch instructor asking if I would take on a friend of hers as a client. The client was a Healing Touch Certified Practitioner. She was moving here to be with her children during her last days. I felt honored that this friend had recommended me. I told her I would be delighted to take the woman as a client and would give her my very best care.

The client and I hit it off the moment we met. She moved into an assisted living place not far from where I lived. We had long discussions about healing, death, and other important moments in life. She was articulate and intelligent. Cancer was attacking her bones. Frequently she was in great pain. I saw her at least once a week and sometimes more often. Energy work does great things to help relieve pain.

One day I answered the phone to find one of her sons on the other end of the line. (I don't use cell phones unless it is an emergency.) His mother had had a heart attack that morning and wasn't expected to survive. They didn't know what to do. Would I please come?

I knew the assisted living people would know what to do. I felt that what the two boys needed was assurance that everything was proceeding properly. It was, of course.

We gathered around her bed. I talked with the boys at length about energy work. It turned out my client hadn't told the boys much about her work as an energy medicine practitioner.

I have a readymade simplistic lecture on energy medicine. Years of practice have reduced it to an elevator speech. The boys got a more detailed version. At the beginning of a healing session a practitioner will do an assessment of the energy system. It doesn't matter which modality the practitioner uses.

As I am fond of saying, "Raykey, Righkey, or Wrongkey, it's all energy work." Reiki, pronounced Raykey, emphasis on the *ray*, is another form of energy work. Because of how it is spelled people don't always know how to pronounce it.

My client rested on her bed. Even though she was breathing very quietly, her breath came and went in a way typical of a person in the coma state that goes with the body shutting down. The boys stood on one side of the bed and I sat in a chair on the other. I decided to demonstrate an assessment to the boys. Her lower chakras were very weak. Her field was full of sparkling, somewhat pastel colors. I liken it to the mist formed around a waterfall, where each droplet has its own tiny rainbow.

Her crown chakra was large and reminded me of a big tomato cage. It rose above her head like a tornado and I could not clearly see the end of it. I didn't tell any of this to the boys. I knew they could not see what I was seeing. I thought I would demonstrate a hand scan and then let them try it.

A hand scan begins about six to eighteen inches above the head. The practitioner moves his or her hand slowly down over the body at a height of six to eight inches above the skin. It ends about twelve inches below the feet. I was in the process of slowly moving my hand down her field when I felt a rippling motion. It felt a little like someone was pulling a blanket out from under my hands. The movement seemed to have started at her feet and moved up her body. When the rippling stopped, I looked at her face. At that moment, she took her last breath. She transitioned so quietly, it took a couple of minutes before her sons realized she had left us.

Her final gift to me was to have me experience her leaving. I know without a doubt she did it on purpose. I am most grateful. She was a terrific teacher.

French philosopher, paleontologist, and Jesuit priest Pierre Teilhard de Chardin says it best, *"We are not human beings having a spiritual experience; we are spiritual beings having a human experience."* I feel my client confirmed that idea. For me, she confirmed we are spirits and that they are separate from our bodies. Actually, I think our bodies are contained within our spirits (or souls if you prefer that term) instead of the other way around. Once the spirit is gone, the body is nothing more than a piece of meat.

I am told there once was a special bed in a local hospital. I don't know if it is still in use. People who were about to make their final transition volunteered to use that bed for their last moments. Everything is weighed, including the breath. Once the body stops functioning, four to five ounces disappear. No one can account for those ounces except to say the soul has left the body.

I have also noticed people die when they choose to. I always thought that when it is time, off you go. To a certain point that is true. However, the exact time of transition varies. People close to leaving may wait until Aunt Matilda shows up so they can say good-bye to each other. Other people have no desire to see Cousin Henry and so they leave before he gets there.

A client brought this concept to my attention. He was in a hospital dying of emphysema. His family stayed with him twenty-four hours a day. They loved him very much and didn't want him to think they were abandoning him during a difficult time. They made sure he was never alone. However, there came a time when one member went out for pizza, another went into a waiting room to talk on her cell phone, and the remaining family member left for a just a minute to use the bathroom. In that quiet few minutes while everyone was gone, he took his last breath and went home.

I arrived a few minutes later. The family was very upset by this. They all blamed each other for leaving him alone. I asked him about it during a quiet moment. Emphysema is not an easy way to die. The struggle for breath is agonizing. The lungs slowly fill with fluid and, in a sense, the patient drowns. This kind man did not want to have his family see him struggle for that last breath and hear the gurgle that went with it. He thought he was doing them a favor. Fortunately, this family is a loving one, and the blaming soon went away and love prevailed.

The point of the story is that he clearly picked his own time to die.

11

Soul Fragments and Other Entities in the Energy Field

The more you struggle and even fail, while you're trying to master new information, the better you're likely to recall and apply that information later.

MANU KAPUR

Having a healing practice provides endless opportunities for learning new things. Intention outweighs technique. Techniques, while fun to learn, don't rule the experience. They merely provide a form of ceremony to remove unwanted congested energy. That energy can come in many forms. I usually see it in the form of dust bunnies cluttering up the energy field. The founder of Healing Touch Program™, Janet Mentgen, saw congested energy as iron filings. Healing Touch provides many techniques for removing congested energy. I use all of them.

Once I master a given technique for removing congested energy, other issues raise their heads. People started coming to me asking for the removal of entities in the energy field, which meant it was time for more study. Several shamanic trainings offer ways to remove entities. When this showed up for the first time, I didn't have the opportunity to find a book that would show me how to remove it. The client was on the table and needed my help. I think my close relationship with my guides began in earnest at this time.

I call my lead guide Oreg. It seems to fit him and he doesn't correct me when I use the name. He doesn't mind when I share it with others. Oreg has never taken human form. To me he looks like a column of sparkling lights, similar to the column of light shown on *Star Trek* when Scotty beams someone on board the Enterprise. Oreg has no gender, but I feel more comfortable referring to him as a male rather than an *it*. I don't know why the masculine terminology, and don't really care.

Oreg coordinates the healing sessions. He tells me he has over three hundred specialized angels and guides available to help. Some specialize in cancer, while others may specialize in relationships, etc. Whatever the client needs, the appropriate unseen helpers come to do the necessary work

The healing begins at the time a client makes an appointment with me. Oreg confers with the client's guides and angels. According to Oreg, angels don't take human form. They like to work with humans because they can learn through the human experiences without having to do it themselves. Being a sentient being on planet Earth is a difficult thing. Angels have a great deal of respect for those of us living here.

Guides have experienced human form in other lifetimes. Guides can provide wise advice for financial issues, while angels are handy when it comes to spiritual questions. I often refer to the term, guides, as meaning both guides and angels. It simplifies things and they don't have egos that care one way or the other. One of my fellow instructors refers to both as unseen helpers. I use that term from time to time.

I have grown to love and respect Oreg very much. He has never steered me wrong. I have misunderstood him at times, which has gotten me into trouble. When that happens, I ask for his advice to come in terminology I can understand. After twenty years of working together we get along rather well from my point of view. He says he agrees with me.

When I do shamanic work, especially concerning the removal of entities in the energy field, I ask one of my angels to form a protective barrier to shield both my client and me from outside influences and to protect the surroundings from whatever gets released. He forms a cone-shaped thing around both of us. It reminds me of the light bulb used in an outside spotlight. The cone starts several feet above my head and comes down to a width of about six or eight feet at the bottom. It curves under my feet going down about eighteen inches into the ground. The narrow top has an opening that leads to the other side of the veil. A guardian angel sits at the opening.

Regarding entities in the human energy field: The first one I encountered looked like a gargoyle found decorating an old building. Portland used to have gargoyles on buildings all over downtown. Unfortunately, most of those beautiful old buildings have succumbed to the wrecking balls. Oreg explained that gargoyles come from another dimension. They eat energy. During a moment of weakness one of these entities can slip into the energy field. I have found them in many different places in the human energy field, but I find most of them angled from the left shoulder with their heads over the heart. We are rich in energy around the heart area.

Even though the entity is nourished by this energy, it is like a human eating grass. It isn't satisfying and it's hard to digest. By removing the entity and sending it home, everybody is happy. I don't know how these creatures end up in our dimension. Oreg says curiosity brings them here, among other things. It is a simple matter to lift one out and hand it over to a guide or an angel to take it home. Usually an unseen helper passes the entity up to the angel sitting at the opening at the top of the cone. Where it goes from there, I don't know.

The client often feels instant relief. The entities have a tendency to encourage their hosts to experience a lot of emotional turmoil, which in turn creates more energy for their lunch. They have weight as well. Many a client has reported feeling lighter after the removal of one of these creatures. I can feel the weight as well. It always amazes me to be picking up something from an energy field that has weight, yet I can't see it. They come in different sizes and weights. Some have been living off their hosts for a long period of time and are more difficult to remove. Newcomers pop right out.

The day came when I found an entity that had human feelings. At first I thought a ghost or guide had attached itself to the client's energy field for some reason, but this wasn't the case. The thing had human feelings, but was way too small to be a ghost or guide. According to Oreg – and I have had this confirmed by others—when a person encounters a truly frightening experience, a piece of themselves separates from the person's field and hides. Many shamans refer to this piece as a soul fragment. I don't think the soul can be broken into fragments. Oreg says it is a part of the personality that breaks away. The individual never feels completely whole once this happens.

The traumatic experience can be as simple as being spanked across the knuckles with a ruler. Usually it comes from a horrific experience such as torture or abuse. The job of the healer or shaman is to find the missing part and blend it back in. Often the missing piece is childlike. It needs reassurance that it is safe to return. The cause is not always known and it usually isn't necessary to discern the cause. The healer comforts the broken fragment and guides it back to its owner. This is done gently, slowly and with great love.

I work with combat veterans at least once a year during a special weekend put on by the Warm Springs tribes here in Oregon. It is a wonderful event and much healing takes place. While working with the veterans, I have noticed lots of soul fragments clinging to the men and women who have seen combat.

What happens to a soul fragment when the person dies

before it can be restored to its person? A good question, and of course Oreg had an answer. The fragment, lost and suddenly very much alone, looks for a compatible human and attaches itself to that person. Combat vets suffering from post-traumatic stress disorder (PTSD) are often covered with them. The soul fragments continue to live in the event that occurred and caused them to flee. Time stops for them.

Working with these soul fragments can be acutely uncomfortable. I have had visions of battle scenes. Sometimes I can smell blood and other yucky stuff that I assume come from battle. Sometimes the feeling of fear is so very intense, I can hardly breathe.

Not all the soul fragments come from soldiers. Innocent bystanders caught in the middle of battle often send out soul fragments. These fragments come home with the soldiers. Fragments don't care which side of the battle a host belongs. I have removed fragments from many Vietnamese people off of American survivors from that war. The same is true for more recent wars. Removal of these fragments, no matter whether they are soldier or civilian, can greatly help a veteran recover from PTSD.

Because the soul fragment is living in the memory of the battle or other trauma of war, it constantly emotes feelings about that event. These feelings leak into the energy field of the host carrying the soul fragments. The host can't get away from them. Constant reminders of battles and other horrors of war stay in the mind of the host. Some soldiers see suicide as the only escape. Soul fragments may encourage this. The host would then take the soul fragments to the other side of the veil, and then hopefully the soul fragment can reunite with its person. The guides do a much better and quicker job of it and, at the same time, free the sufferer of PTSD from some of the guilt, horror, and other such feelings carried home from war.

Once I release a soul fragment, one of the guides carries it up to the opening at the top of the cone. I can frequently see a person waiting for it. Sometimes I sense a joyous reunion. Other times the fragment passes through the opening and moves on. I once released eighty-seven fragments from a combat veteran. The guy was a big man and filled a doorway when he walked through it. He was also a strong man, a leader in his community, and didn't put up with nonsense. I don't remember which war he fought in. It was one of those times when I could sense and feel the horrors of battle. I can't help but wonder how people can live through such trauma and keep their sanity.

He went into shock after the last entity left his body. The Native Americans (many were firefighters and knew first aid) treated him for shock and I left the room. I was a little tired from the ordeal and sat in a living room chatting with some of the women there. A short while later he entered the living room flapping both his arms and laughing.

He cried out, "I feel so light!"

We all felt his joy.

Things happen during battles which no sane person would even dream in their worst nightmares. Sometimes innocent people are killed or injured during moments of pure insanity. There was a time when I was judgmental and felt people should have more control. During a heated battle, all stops are pulled. Things happen so fast a person has no time to think about what he or she is doing. The guilt carried by soldiers after such events is overwhelming and not often talked about. It shows up in the energy field, and a good practitioner can help clear away the congested energy carrying those emotions caught up in the field.

Sometimes the actions taking place in a battle are part of agreements made before the parties came to Earth. I know that sounds a little far-fetched. For people to participate in a prearranged meeting in a faraway place sounds like predestination and takes away from free will. It doesn't. How each person interacts in a given event, such as a battle, can change the agreement or not. Each person participating, and it can be more than two, has choice. Sometimes a person chooses to opt out of the agreement and may not even show up. The agreement does not dictate the outcome. It merely provides an opportunity for each participant to do whatever it is they wanted to do, be it to learn something, to test themselves in a given situation, or bring balance to their existence. The possibilities are endless.

In recent years, something else showed up. Snakes. Snakes began appearing in the energy fields of Vietnam combat veterans. They come in threes. Removal of these snakes is tricky and requires a lot of help from the guides. I don't recommend removing snakes unless the practitioner has a really good relationship with his or her guides and can understand and follow their directions exactly.

I wondered why I was suddenly seeing these snakes and only in Vietnam combat veterans. I got an answer the following year after I first began removing snakes from several combat veterans attending the Warm Springs healing event.

One of the men went to Vietnam for a visit soon after I had removed snakes from his field. He met with some Vietnamese shamans while there. The subject of the snakes came up. Apparently at some point during the war, some Vietnamese shamans got together and placed a curse on the soldiers invading their country, specifically Americans. The snakes were a result of the curse. The shamans who created the curses have mostly died. The reasons for the curses no longer have any power, and they have weakened considerably. Thus, they are now ready for removal and are showing up in the energy fields of the combat veterans here in the United States.

Three is considered an unlucky number in Vietnam, which is why the snakes always come in threes. Some of the vets have reported back to me that diabetes and other abdominal disorders improved after the removal of snakes.

I once saw a snake with its teeth embedded in a pancreas. The man had a severe case of diabetes. Unfortunately, the veteran had lived with diabetes for over forty years. He was so used to the disease, he couldn't let go of it. I don't know if his A1C dropped or not. (A1C stands for glycated hemoglobin. The A1C test gives a measure of how much sugar is attached to the blood's hemoglobin protein over a two- to three-month period.) I haven't seen him since we did the healing work together. I do know he is still with us.

12

A New Experience

*Funny how it usually takes imminent death
or tragedy to think about life in light of eternity,
but that's what got me willing to explore.*

John Burke

A dear friend of mine is a real estate agent. She had a listing for a house that had been on the market for several months. It was a nice house in a good location. The price was right, but for some reason it wasn't selling.

She approached me one day about the problem. She said she noticed a presence whenever she entered the house and wondered if perhaps something was there that didn't want the house to be sold. She thought it might be some energy left behind after the owners moved out.

I had learned a technique to clear energy fields. One of my instructors once mentioned the technique could be used to clear buildings as well. I thought it might be fun to give it a try.

I walked through the house looking for congested energy. I used the technique to clear each room and then brought in white healing light to fill all the spaces I had emptied. I found congestion in two areas I couldn't account for. It didn't clear when I did the technique. I thought about it for a while. With a little nudge from one of my unseen helpers, I sat down on the floor in the middle of the living room.

I gained a very important tool when I took the PSI Basic class from PSI World. They taught me how to build a workshop in my mind. Within the workshop I placed a window, which PSI World calls *the screen of the mind*. I use it all daily.

Using the screen of the mind, I visualized every room in the house. Even though the house was empty I could see furniture on the screen. In a bedroom, I saw a double bed with an old woman sleeping there. When I visualized going into the room, I saw the lady was no longer sleeping. She died there. Her spirit had moved on. However, a little of her energy stayed behind and I cleared it. The room immediately seemed much brighter.

A New Experience

In the living room sat an elderly man in a wheel chair. He was keeping vigil for the lady in the bedroom. His spirit was still there. I talked with him. He didn't want to cross over because he felt he was responsible to watch over the lady in the bedroom. His chair was placed so that he could see her.

I told him she had passed on. A quizzical look came in to his eyes. I explained that time had stopped for him. What he thought he was seeing didn't exist in present time. She was no longer there. The family had moved and the house was up for sale. His presence was preventing it from selling.

"What am I doing here then!" he exclaimed.

At that point, a beam of white light came down beside him. He got up out of the chair and walked into the light. The light left taking him with it.

It seemed like the house sighed and a sense of peace came over the building. It sold three days later.

This event took place long before I had my near-death experience. I wondered what I had done. I have read lots of stories of the white light. None of them were quite like what I had just seen. I felt like the lady in the TV series, *The Ghost Whisperer*. The only difference was that my ghost wasn't very talkative and he didn't offer a passionate thank you for setting him free. But then, at that point I really didn't think I had done anything. I wondered if it was all in my imagination.

Later, my friend told me the old man had made his transition first. The old woman died later. His spirit did not know of the passage of time. To his spirit, everything stayed the same. He remained behind to guard her. Because he was caught in the time of his own death, he was unaware that she had made her transition at a later time. Once he understood his reason for staying on Earth no longer existed, he was able to go home via the white light.

I have heard stories of mischievous ghosts that like to tease people or frighten them. I've also heard stories where ghosts have deliberately warded off potential buyers for a house or other building, because they didn't like the intrusion of strangers in the building.

I personally have never met one to do any of these things deliberately. All of the ones that I have come in contact with have had their own agendas. They were oblivious to their surroundings or the passage of time.

I still don't know why the old man didn't see the woman's spirit leave. I have wondered why she didn't tell him. My guides say that the old man was locked in his own world of how things should be. As a result, he never saw the changes. They also told me the woman left directly when it came her time. She was unaware of the man guarding her.

I have come to trust my guides. They have never lied to me. If I ignore them, I often get myself into trouble. I don't always understand what they say to me, which can get me into trouble, too. I now ask questions. In the beginning, I was so sure I was imagining all of it. Now that there have been so many experiences validated, I have no doubts.

13

The Professor's House

No one wants to leave the planet in a state of discord with his or her family. We are all going to reach the departure lounge—one day. Will you be ready?

DAVID BRADY

We had such good results with the first house, my real estate friend wanted me to help with another problem. She had sold a house to someone in another town. The lady loved the house, but shortly after she moved in, she sensed a dark presence in the place. Even though the house was in a sunny location, it seemed dark and dreary to her. A short while later she began to have nightmares. Gigantic shrimp were threatening her. She felt like they were chasing her even in daylight. Now this was a very down-to-earth, no nonsense woman. She has a PhD and teaches at a local university.

She called for help. My real estate friend told her about my clearing the first house of a ghost and thought I might be able to help her. By this time, the lady was desperate. She couldn't bear going home, and was staying with a friend for a few days.

We set up an appointment for me to come check out the house. The lady would be at work, but she said she would leave a key under the mat. I arrived around two in the afternoon. It was a cloudy day. I found the key and went into the house. Dark menacing energy was everywhere.

It seemed to me there had to be a reason for it. I explored the house looking for the source and couldn't find it. I sat down in the living room to meditate on the subject. The front door was behind me and another door to the back patio faced me. The back door was mostly glass. I looked through the glass and saw a lady in her late forties sunbathing in the back patio. She had on white shorts and a halter top that reminded me of a movie from the 1950s. I can remember my mother wearing clothes like that when I was young.

Behind me, the weather was cloudy. This lady, lying on a reclining chair in the back patio, was in full sun. In my reality it was March, too cold for sunbathing. It took

The Professor's House

me a few minutes to realize I was looking at a ghost, not a live person.

I wanted to know why she was haunting the house and so I asked her.

"I'm mad at my children. They don't appreciate anything I do for them. They ignore me most of the time. I have been sick for a long time and they don't believe me when I tell them I am in pain. I want them to suffer. After I had my heart attack I decided I would stay and make life miserable for them," she answered.

"Are you aware the house has sold?"

"It has?" she said.

"Yes," I said. "And your children moved away a long time ago."

"Oh," she said. "I guess there is no reason for me to stay."

With that, the white light came down and she disappeared. I used my clearing technique to rid the house of all the dark energy. I had to clear out closets, built-in chests of drawers, the bathroom, kitchen cabinets, and all the rooms. When I left, I felt the house had a light, happier feeling to it. I thought it might be my imagination, but it seemed like the house itself brightened when the ghost left.

I got a phone call the next day. When the new owner arrived home, she thought she might be in the wrong house. It was so much brighter. It felt warm and inviting to her. Later on, she called the real estate agent to say she no longer had nightmares. We never did find out why gigantic shrimp showed up in her dreams and later chased her around the house. I don't think the ghost created the shrimp either. I have no answers for that one.

However, I found out later the ghost's children had abused her verbally. They didn't want to deal with her illness and ignored it. They gave her a pretty bad time about it. It saddens me to see how our actions can influence another's thinking. We all know obnoxious people. There seems to be one in every family. After a while people tend to ignore or avoid such people. Sick people are really suffering in ways we can't imagine. People with chronic diseases do need a lot of patience and love, and it isn't always easy to give it to them. I am no exception. However, I would rather be the one offering comfort than the one receiving it. When I get impatient with someone who has a chronic issue, I remind myself that I am glad it isn't me wearing their shoes. It makes it easier for me to offer comfort, rather than be critical and judgmental.

My mother has a form of dementia and it is often troublesome for me to be patient and kind, when I would really like to smack her a good one and tell her to get on with the program. I am learning a lot about the dying process from her. She is taking her sweet time about it. Most of the time, that is okay. But every once in a while, when the same problem keeps recurring, I feel impatient and have to really pounce on myself to stay kind and even friendly.

14

A Miscarriage

Most people struggle with letting go of someone who left his or her life. This could be from death or simply other circumstances.

KELLIE SULLIVAN

My realtor friend was very happy with me. It became a regular thing for me to clear a house that didn't sell. I was still a bit skeptical about the whole thing, and I couldn't help but think I had an overactive imagination. Admittedly, I did not know about the elderly couple in the first house. That information came a couple of days later. I also couldn't explain why the new owner of the last house thought her new home went from a dark and dreary, somewhat frightening place to one of sunlight and happiness.

I even toyed with the notion that I should quit while I was ahead. None of this fit into my Christian background of how the afterlife works. I had so many questions. The next house only added to my confusion.

My friend, the real estate agent, called again. This time she had a house that had been on the market for months. They had lowered the price a couple of times, and it still hadn't sold. Would I please come and clear the house? She couldn't even get clients to come look at it.

Reluctantly I agreed. This time there was a difference. My real estate friend led the study group I mentioned earlier. A dozen or so women attended the study group each month. I was one of them. We have read a number of books together including *A Course in Miracles*. We were all seekers looking for understanding as to how healing works, the universe functions, and how to communicate with guides, angels, and other unseen helpers, among other things.

Many in the group wanted to know how we can raise the vibration of the planet. I am not sure that is necessary. However, it is a popular subject. People wanting to do the work have good intentions and sincerely want to help all people regardless of actions, race, creed, or sexual orientation. When I am working on a spiritual level, those labels don't exist.

My realtor friend invited the group of women to come and be a part of the clearing. She thought they might be able to help. Five of them came to help clear the house of dark congested energy. The group sat in a circle on the floor of the dining area in the house. I think my friend led them in a meditation to help brighten the inside of the house. They planned to channel the dark energies into a crystal bowl, a technique someone had recently learned.

At last, I thought, I would have witnesses to validate what I saw. As it turned out they never noticed what I found.

The house was empty of all furniture and belongings. The previous owner had suffered from cancer for twelve years before her transition. Evidence of her pain and sorrow filled the house with a dark sense of foreboding.

I did my physical exploring thing. I even went into attic over the garage. The only place I found unusual energy was in a small bedroom at the front of the house. I felt this was the source of the problem. I sat down in the middle of the bedroom and closed my eyes. I went over every inch of the house using my screen of the mind to do the searching. I found nothing until I came back into the room where I was sitting. There I saw a woman in a rocking chair. She was crying.

"May I help you?" I said.

"I can't find my baby," she answered.

I looked for the baby everywhere. I knew it was somewhere in the house. After finding nothing, but sensing that it was still there somewhere, I got up off the floor and began searching. I looked in all the rooms and all the closets.

It figures. The last closet I checked was in the room where I had been meditating and found the woman. There in the closet was a tiny baby wrapped in a small blanket lying in a doll's carriage. The baby was so small, I thought it must have been either a miscarriage or premature birth. What I still find intriguing is that the baby's spirit wasn't there, yet the image was. I think the lady may have hidden the little body there after she either miscarried, had a very early premature birth, or possibly aborted it. Some of the baby's essence was barely present, but the baby's spirit had moved on.

The woman looked at the empty closet. She could see there was nothing left.

"I think my baby has gone to Heaven," she said.

She looked at me sadly. "Do you think I will see her again?"

I nodded my head, yes.

"Then I guess I am ready too," she said.

With that, the white light came down and she was gone.

I asked my women's group to shine golden, white light

all through the house to help rid it of the sadness that lingered there. They did a good job. In the next few days, seven clients came to look at the house. Even though it was a down market at the time, it sold four days later for cash and closed within a week.

15

Two Ghosts

Further complicating grandparents' grief is the horrible reality that a young person died before they did. Children aren't supposed to die before their parents, and they certainly are not supposed to die before their grandparents.

ALAN D. WOLFEL

I fell in love with the next house that had problems. It's located in a nearby town. It's old and large. I have always been attracted to older homes. They have so much history. It's as though they have been blessed by many families' lives. I can almost hear the laughter and love in an old house. I have always felt this way.

When I first saw this house, I was captivated. If I could have afforded it, I would have bought it on the spot. Once inside though, I knew it had problems. My real estate friend thought the spirit of a mentally ill girl still remained in the house.

I had great fun exploring the house. It had three stories of rooms full of nooks and crannies. A very large, old oak tree guarded the property. Lilacs and other lovelies decorated the yard. Even though it was the middle of winter, the grounds and the house were still beautiful.

I noticed the oak tree was ill. How I knew this I don't know. I decided to do some healing work on the tree. I hugged it for quite a while. I later learned the tree leafed out in its full glory that spring.

It took me a while to find the mentally ill girl. I knew she was somewhere near the kitchen. I finally found her hidden in a closet off the kitchen. The house had had some remodeling work done after the passing of the child. The closet now contained the laundry space. I don't know what was there during the girl's lifetime, possibly a butler's pantry.

It took a bit of comforting to get her to trust me. She spoke gibberish. I have no idea what she meant to say. I do know she was very frightened. I brought the light down and guided her to it. Something inside the light beckoned to her and she joyfully embraced it. The light disappeared and so did she.

I felt like my work was not yet done. I knew there was

another presence somewhere in the house. The spirit of the girl was so dominant, I missed this one when I first explored the house. This spirit was not very strong, at least in the way it presented itself to me. I even looked outside the building to see if it was nearby. I found it while I was spreading healing white light throughout the house.

After a second pass inside the house, I finally discovered it in the living room. I saw a man sitting in an easy chair. He told me he was watching over his granddaughter. He was frustrated because he didn't know how to communicate with her. He very much wanted to help her. He had stayed behind when his body gave out, because of his concern for the girl. He didn't want her to be alone with strangers. He knew they frightened her.

I told him she had made her transition a long time ago. He looked at me like I was crazy. I then told him about her spirit that I found hiding in the closet off the kitchen. I assured him she had moved on. He gave a sigh of relief, the light came down, and he was gone.

I find it frustrating in cases like this one. The person moves into the light and disappears and I don't get to hear the whole story.

Sometimes family can fill in some details. Most of the time the family doesn't even know I have been to their house.

The real estate agent can ask questions as she also wants

to know what happened. However, I sometimes get information that the family doesn't want made public, and here we are asking questions about things we have no right to know.

It gets tricky.

16

My Mother-in-Law's Transition

Many fear talking about it because they have no clue about life after death. They know not where they go after their death. Is it heaven, hell, or some other place? However, fear cannot stop death from coming.

VINCENT KMC

In my experiences with ghosts, I have found three reasons why a ghost doesn't cross over: not realizing they have died, having an earthly agenda, and fear of going to Hell. There are probably dozens more, but I have a feeling they would be variations of the three I mentioned. I encountered the last reason when my mother-in-law made her transition. In my not-so-humble opinion, the fear of going to Hell is the saddest of the three.

I got the call from my sister-in-law that my mother-in-law was about to leave us. I rushed to the assisted living place where she was staying. My mother-in-law has three daughters and a son. Two of her daughters live locally and were at their mother's side when I got there. One lived in New York and was not present. Her son, my wusband, was delayed by an accident on the freeway. It took quite a while to go around it. He finally arrived about twenty minutes after his mother made her transition.

We three women stayed by her bedside. My mother-in-law was aware of what was happening. it was clear to us that she was very frightened. Her daughters assured her that it was time for her to go, and gave their approval of her doing so. I felt I was there more to support them than I was for my mother-in-law.

I could see my mother-in-law was fighting hard to stay alive. She was very much afraid of what was going on. Whatever reassurance her daughters gave her fell on deaf ears. She did not want to make her transition. It seemed to me when the time finally came, that her body simply stopped functioning. I did not see her spirit leave her body. In fact, I felt its presence quite strongly even after the body stopped breathing.

My wusband made a bit of a fuss about not being there

in time. I would have, too, if I had been in his shoes. Actually, I think he was secretly relieved. He is a very tender-hearted man. It pained him greatly to lose his mother, even though he knew it was the right thing for her.

My mother-in-law's quarters were quite spacious for an assisted living place. Each little apartment consisted of a small living room with a separate bedroom and bathroom. We all assembled in the living room to discuss what needed to happen next.

I kept going back into the bedroom where my mother-in-law's body lay on the bed. I had this strong feeling she was still there. I half expected her to open her eyes and indicate in some small way that she was still among the living. The body never moved. The feeling was so strong, I decided I needed to do something about it. When I got home, I sat in the middle of my living room floor. and through the use of the screen of my mind, went back in my mother-in-law's room. By that time her body had been taken by the mortuary people. The furniture was still there as it was too late in the day for the family to move it away. The cleaning crew had not been in the room because they were waiting for us to remove all of her belongings before they cleaned and sterilized the room.

I found my mother-in-law sitting on her bed. I could see that she was terrified. I can only guess as to why. (Oreg had his own opinions.) Her father had been raised in a Southern Baptist Church. Hellfire and brimstone were popular topics coming from the pulpit. I have often wondered if people are entranced by horrific visions of Hell, and that it makes for good entertainment in church. At least it does until it is transition time.

My mother-in-law was raised in a popular, traditional protestant church. Hellfire and brimstone were not topics of sermons. I attended her church off and on for a number of years after I married her son. I think some of the fear of Hell had trickled down from her father when she was a small child. It certainly didn't come from the ministers of this church.

My mother-in-law was one of the kindest people I have ever met. I never once heard her speak ill of anyone. She might have disagreed with someone's actions or ideas. Those she would speak about. But never did she say anything unkind or degrading about anyone. The only way we knew she was in pain was when she would put her hand behind her back to ease discomfort there. She never once complained, even in her later years while suffering from dementia.

This is the last person I would have thought to have a fear of where she was going in the afterlife. In my mind, I held her for a while. I talked softly about family waiting for her. In her fear, she could not see all the beings waiting for her to transition. They were all around us.

I saw the white light a few feet away from her. She didn't want to look at it. I didn't know what to do. One of my guides suggested I go into the light and walk the light to her. I did so. I reached out and took her hands and pulled her into the light with me. At that moment both the white light and my mother-in-law disappeared. I was left alone standing in an empty room. Even the beings that had come to greet her had disappeared. The strong feeling of her presence was gone. She never came back. I checked several times. I love her dearly and know she is happy where she is now.

17

Roseburg

*Death—especially when unexpected—has a way of wiping
away the filters we've put on our lives and giving us
a new perspective about where we are
and where we may be headed.*

A. C. ASEH

The Veterans Administration provided a grant for nurses wanting to study Healing Touch. The student who made his transition described in Chapter Eight spoke often about Healing Touch and how beneficial it was for pain and stress relief. His nutritionist talked with him about it a lot. She applied for a grant and started a movement across the country. Classes are still being taught today in various veteran's hospitals. I have seen people with post-traumatic stress disorders go through miraculous changes after receiving Healing Touch and other biofield therapies.

I was asked to teach a class in southern Oregon. It was a bit awkward. Instead of a nice room with plenty of space for massage tables used in healing, we were placed in a house on the grounds. I think it was originally intended as officer quarters, but was not being used that way anymore. The living room contained a lot of furniture which made it quite crowded when we set up the massage tables for students' use to practice techniques on each other. We managed.

All of us had fun exploring the house. The main floor consisted of a living room, a dining room, and a kitchen, and two sunrooms at each end of the house. The house had four bedrooms and two bathrooms upstairs. We had no access to the basement. The attic was a large unfinished and empty space. I knew the house was haunted.

On the second day, while the students were practicing on each other and had little need for me at the moment, I went into my meditative state and searched the house for ghosts. I encountered two.

The first ghost was a darling little old lady. I found her in one of the upstairs bedrooms. She had on a flowered print dress with a cream background. A small hat with tiny flowers in the brim sat on top of her head. She held a small purse in front of her. She looked like she was waiting for a bus. I talked to her and could see she was quite confused. She didn't answer me. I don't think she knew she had died.

The white light was to her left. She ignored it. I reached for her hand, and she gave it to me quite willingly. I felt like she needed help, as she didn't seem to know where to go. I guided her to the light and she left.

The second ghost I found in the attic. He was sitting on the floor, leaning against a wall. I have no idea why he was there or even how he got there. It looked like someone had drawn a line diagonally from the top of his head down to the left of his chest. Above the line his body was blistered and oozing fluids, as though from a bad burn. Below the line, he seemed to be fine. I got the impression he had been hit with a flame thrower or something like one. The burns must have been excruciatingly painful. He rocked back and forth trying to comfort himself.

My first thought was that I was imagining him. There was a diagonal line on the fireplace across the room from where I sat. I opened my eyes to check it out. The diagonal lines were different. The fireplace line was only six inches or so long. The line on the man's body was much longer and more ragged.

In spite of all the validations of work I had done before, I still had doubts about the work I was doing.

The white light was situated in front of the man and a little to his left. I tried to talk with him, but all he could do to answer was moan. His mouth was so covered with blisters I don't think he could form words.

I told him the white light was waiting for him. He never looked up. I decided my only course of action was to step into the light and walk it over to him. I did so, held out my hands to him, and said, "You will find some comfort here."

He looked at me standing in the light, my hands reaching down to him. He reached up with his one good hand and took one of my hands. Together we got him into a standing position in the light and he disappeared, taking the light with him.

New questions arose. Why didn't these two people know they had died? Because they didn't know, why didn't loved ones who had gone before, communicate with them to let them know the light was waiting for them?

The only thing I can think of was that neither ghost recognized their situation. The sweet little lady probably had dementia. She was living in her own world and wasn't noticing anything going on around her. She didn't know she had guardian angels. If she heard them beckoning to her to come to the light, she probably ignored them.

The soldier was so caught up in his physical misery he

didn't notice he had died either. The agony that filled his mind blocked out any other sensations. He failed to recognize his surroundings or the passage of time. I suspect physical injuries were not the only things to hold him there. How he got into the attic of this house was another unanswered question. I would like to know.

Guardian angels cannot help unless they are asked. Otherwise they interfere with free will. I think loved ones who have transitioned earlier, either cannot leave the white light or they must abide by the accords and cannot help without being asked. I can see where this rule can be a problem at times, especially when the human doesn't know about it. I haven't come across a better explanation.

18

A Dog's Transition

Dogs come into our lives to teach us about love, they depart to teach us about loss. A new dog never replaces an old dog, it merely expands the heart. If you have loved many dogs, your heart is very big.

ERICA JONG

My mother's dog, Tibby, had been ill for some time. My mother was unable to make a decision concerning whether it was time to put him down. When she fell, broke her hip, and had to be hospitalized, I took over care of the dog.

His hind feet could not support him. He had no control over his bowels and urinary tract. He was having trouble eating, and frequently threw up his meals. I knew something was very wrong.

Instead of taking Tibby home with me, I took him to my veterinarian. I didn't like what my mother was telling me about what her veterinarian had to say. I don't know if what she said was actually what the vet recommended, or an adulteration to fit her desires for the dog. I wanted to know what was really going on in Tibby's body. I also took him to the vet because I lived in a rental house and couldn't keep a dog that wasn't able to go outside to do his doggy duties.

The vet took one look at Tibby and recognized a neurological condition. He tested the dog and confirmed his initial diagnosis. I left the dog at the veterinary clinic while I went to confer with my mother about putting him down. She wanted to see him one last time.

I took Tibby to see Mother at the rehab center where she was recovering from the partial hip replacement resulting from her fall. Tibby wasn't very responsive to her. I had brought him into the facility in a plastic dog carrier. It is a good thing I did, because he made a big mess. Fortunately, most of it stayed in the dog carrier. It wasn't easy to clean using only the paper towels provided by the rehab center. Mother finally agreed it was time to let him go.

I took Tibby back to the vet. We set an appointment for the next day for the vet to put him down. I arrived in tears and held Tibby throughout the whole procedure. To begin the procedure, the doctor gave the dog a shot to make him sleepy. Apparently, some dogs panic in the last moment when their heart stops. By making them go to sleep ahead of time, they do not experience that moment of panic and it makes their passing easier.

Tibby got his sleepy shot. He fought it at first and then settled down with a sigh. It sounded like a sigh of relief to me. The doctor said he would be back in half an hour. I sat quietly with Tibby, crying the whole time. I talked to him about what a good dog he had been, and that it was time to go home. After a while I heard him sigh, and saw his spirit leave his body, which surprised me. I wasn't expecting that.

A few seconds later the veterinarian entered the room to give the dog his final shot. I wasn't sure he needed it after having seen Tibby's spirit leave. The vet listened to his heart and it was still beating. I thought of my stepfather leaving long before his body quit working. It felt to me like something similar was happening here. The doctor gave Tibby his final shot and the dog's heart quit beating almost immediately.

I looked at the vet and saw tears in his eyes. I have always liked him. He exhibited a great love of animals and showed them respect, a trait not always present. I thanked him. He had me sit with Tibby for a while. All was quiet. Tibby was long gone. I called for the veterinarian's assistant to come get Tibby's body and left.

No one can tell me dogs and other animals do not have spirits. I have found all things, including rocks, have an energy field of some kind. However, Tibby turned out to be another one of my teachers. Leaving his body the way he did, he confirmed my suspicions that animals have souls of their own. I do not know if they go where we go in the afterlife. I suspect there are connections.

I cannot see animals, mammals especially, as lesser beings as they are easier for me to form a connection. They have their reasons for coming here. They know ahead of time their lives are different from ours. Animals, such as cattle and chickens, know they are coming in as a source of food. Saying grace is a nice thing. I like the Native American practice of thanking both the animals and the plants for providing food that we might live.

It's a dog-eat-dog world. Every living thing provides food for other living beings from the biggest whale to the smallest microbe. It goes on in the peaceful nature scenes we love so much even if we can't see it at the moment. Animals are eating plants and, depending upon the species, other animals. Birds are eating bugs. Some plants capture and eat bugs, often in a very unpleasant and slow way. Bugs are eating plants and dead animals. Some bugs feed on live animals. I'd like to talk to whoever created mosquitoes, fleas, ticks, etc. Ahem. Enough said.

It is more obvious when we see a lion take down a deer on TV. Violence is everywhere in nature. It is not just a human experience. We see cows being slaughtered and think it is inhumane in the way it is done. I have often thought the fright a deer feels when confronted by a mountain lion is no different than the feelings of a pig about to be slaughtered. I am not sure I understand this interrelationship.

I have recently learned wild animals have a sense of when they are about to die. An agreement is formed between the predator and the prey. Their spirits leave just before they are killed by a predator. If it is not their time as prey, no agreement is made, and they escape the predator.

The hunters of many indigenous cultures do make an agreement ahead of time. They call for an animal to come to them as a volunteer. An animal who is ready to go home then shows up. Domesticated animals do not have the opportunity to make an agreement. Unconscious personnel frighten the animals and fear taints their blood with adrenaline.

The learning opportunities are tremendous. Maybe that is what it is all about.

19

Some Other Experiences

*When you are sorrowful look again in your heart,
and you shall see that in truth you are weeping
for that which has been your delight.*

KAHLIL GIBRAN

I have had unexpected encounters with ghosts while playing the role of a tourist. I ran into a ghost while on an underground tour in Portland Oregon. I was about to cross over a glass covered pit leading to an opening in a basement of a large building downtown. The glass was there to preserve the essence of the town as it was, without the danger of someone falling into the pit.

As I walked by, I saw the ghost of an elderly Chinese man sitting in the bottom of the pit. He looked quite forlorn. I could sense he felt lost and very alone. I caught his attention. He expressed surprise that I could see him.

I pointed to the light. He frowned, not knowing what it was for. I couldn't get to him and didn't know what to do. I wasn't in a position to go into a meditative state to work with him. The tour guide wanted us to move on. Then I had an idea. I asked his guardian angel to help him go into the light. A few seconds later the Chinaman disappeared. Please remember, angels and guides cannot take action unless we ask them to. That is why the guardian angel had to wait until I asked it to, before it could help the man cross into the light.

In the far northwest corner of Oregon is a delightful town full of old houses. A friend and I decided to visit one of the old houses that had been preserved as a museum. Tourists could visit during the day. Before we went inside, we stopped to watch a movie about the family that had lived there over a hundred years ago.

Volunteers told the stories of the early history of the region. Much of the movie was about the sea captain who built the house. He died shortly after it was finished. He spent very little time there. His daughters inherited the house. They lived in the house with their families. One of them never married.

After signing the guest register, we began to poke around.

The main drawing room was roped off. It was the only room barring access. Even though the sun shone through the windows, the room appeared dreary.

We moved off and I told my friend I thought the house was haunted. Because it was old, she agreed it was a distinct possibility. We explored the house and had a great time. I didn't find the ghost at first, even though I knew it was around somewhere.

As we were leaving, I took a last look in the drawing room. There was the ghost, a middle-aged woman sitting on a settee. She didn't look happy to me. She saw me looking at her and said, "What are you doing in my house?"

I explained, "This is no longer your house. A hundred years have passed. It has been sold to the city and is now a museum."

"I want to be left alone to study my music," she said ignoring my comment. I had noticed a grand piano in the room. There was a music stand nearby. It was a very big room.

"Do you play the piano?" I asked.

She nodded her head.

I looked around the room and came back to her when I heard her sigh. She was frowning. "They're gone, aren't they?" she asked. I took that to mean her family.

"Yes," I said. "They left a long, long time ago."

"I am so tired," she said.

"There is a white light in front of you," I said. "Can you see it?"

"Yes," she said. "I want it to come nearer. I am too tired to walk over there."

With that comment said, the light moved over her and both the woman and the light disappeared.

A lady volunteer sat in the hall at the registration table. My friend had struck up a conversation with her while I was busy sending the ghost home. After it left, the lady commented on the sunshine now lighting up the area. It came in through the windows of the drawing room adjacent to where she sat. Two sets of double wide doors opened out into the hall allowing visitors to view the drawing room.

"You almost never see sunlight in that room," she commented as we were preparing to leave. "It's usually a dark and gloomy room." We didn't tell the woman what I had done.

After we left the building, my friend told me about her conversation with the volunteer. The ghost was one of the sea captain's daughters. She was the one who never married. She studied music for much of her lifetime and rarely left the drawing room except for meals and sleeping.

A Mortgage Problem

There is a sacredness in tears.
They are not the mark of weakness, but of power.
They speak more eloquently than ten thousand tongues.
They are the messengers of overwhelming grief,
of deep contrition, and of unspeakable love.

WASHINGTON IRVING

A friend of mine wanted to buy a house. Never had she encountered so many obstacles to obtaining a simple loan. She had a substantial down payment and no outstanding or unpleasant debts. Her job paid well. She tried several loan companies and either got turned down on the spot or experienced nuisance requirements and long delays. Even the title company delayed proceedings and made some mistakes that caused grief with the loan companies.

Finally, she called me. I had once shared with her some of my house-clearing stories. She wanted to know if it was possible that a ghost was interfering with the sale of the house. The house itself was over a hundred years old. It had been remodeled a few times, and an entire wing had been added onto the house. She felt a presence in the area that she and her fiancé were planning to change into a large bedroom.

The earnest agreement was about to run out. She didn't want to lose the house and would have been very upset if she had to forego the earnest money. I couldn't get over to see the house that day. In desperation, she sent me a picture of the house by email.

I saw the problem almost immediately. Looking out of an upstairs window was the face of an elderly man. He appeared at first glance to be quite cranky as he seemed to be scowling. However, the field around him made me think of someone who was lonely and afraid. I went into the workshop of my mind and brought him in. We talked for a while.

His children had placed him on the second floor. He couldn't walk and had to sit in a wheelchair most of his days. Because he was upstairs, he was left alone and often forgotten. They brought him meals and helped him to the bathroom from time to time. Unfortunately, there were times when they left the house, or simply forgot about him. Those were the times when he soiled himself. He felt very ashamed of himself when he lost control. Of course, that upset his kids and made things worse.

Strangers scared him. He was afraid he might soil himself while they were there. He also had trouble speaking. The connection between what he wanted to say and what came out of his mouth didn't always work right. It frustrated him. He desperately wanted to be understood.

He yelled at his children a lot. It wasn't that he liked to yell. He thought it was the only way he could get their attention. When they couldn't understand him, everyone got upset. Most times he just gave up and sat in his chair looking out the window.

As a result, he did not want the house sold. All the strangers running through the house bothered him no end. They talked about making changes to his house. He liked things just the way they were. All the interruptions to his peace and quiet made him quite grumpy.

I asked him, "Do you know you have died?"

"I have?" He seemed very surprised.

"Yes," I said. "Your children have moved on. Someone else owns the house now. They are most anxious to sell it."

"Well, I'll be. What d'you know about that? What do I do now?"

"See the light there in front of you?"

"Yeah. It's been kind of a nuisance, blocking my view of the street at times."

"Step into the light," I said.

"Now why would I wanna do a thing like that? Besides, in case you haven't noticed, I ain't stepping anywhere."

He had me there. I thought about his dilemma for a moment.

"Call the light to you," I suggested.

"Why?" he said.

I was afraid his crankiness would take over and make things more difficult. Then I got an idea. I said, "You asked for peace and quiet. You'll find it in the light."

"You're sure about that?"

"Yes, I am sure. I also think you'll find people who truly love you waiting for you there."

"Trudy?"

"I don't know. But I think it's worth a try, and it can't hurt you."

No matter what I said, he still didn't want to go into the light. I tried walking the light to him. He backed away. I gave up and talked to his guardian angel. The angel suggested I back off as this man did not want to be forced into anything. I settled back and watched.

The guardian angel went over to the man and talked with him a while. From the way they spoke to each other, I could tell they knew each other well. Soon the light came down, and they both disappeared.

The next morning my friend got a call to say that her loan had cleared, and soon after that the title company was ready to close. She moved in a week later.

21

The Lawyer

*Death in itself is nothing; but we fear to be
we know not what, we know not where.*

JOHN DRYDEN

Of all of my experiences with clearing houses this one is my favorite. It helped reassure me that what I saw and heard while talking with a ghost wasn't just my imagination.

A friend called. She, too, had heard my stories. She owns a gorgeous three story house in an older part of town. My friend had checked out the history of the home and discovered that she was the fifth owner. The house was built by a fairly well-to-do man who owned a large grocery store in the neighborhood. He built the house for his two spinster daughters.

My friend had lived in the house for over twenty years. Even on the sunniest of days the house always seemed to be dark and gloomy on the inside. It had lots of windows on the south side of the house. She felt it should be brighter. Sometimes at night she could feel a presence and wondered if one of the former owners still remained in the house. She had company coming to stay for a few days. Her friends had been there before and had commented on the gloominess of the place. She thought if I rid the house of whatever presence or dark energy that lingered, it would brighten up the place and her friends would feel more welcome.

I was delighted to be offered a tour of the house. I loved it. It had a huge living room and dining room. Off the dining room was a sunroom. The kitchen was unusually small for such a large house. My mother was the one who told us about kitchens being in the basement in the early days. Sometime later in the house's history, the kitchen replaced the butler's pantry on the main level of the house.

We started in the basement. It was dark in the basement with plenty of room. There weren't many windows and the ones there were small. It was a normal basement for a house that age and size. The second floor had four bedrooms and a bath. The third floor was all one room. Someone had finished the attic and made it livable. It had lots of south-facing windows. It was also quite bright and cheerful. I asked my friend if it was always this way.

"Yes," she answered. "If I feel down because of the dreariness, I come up here."

We went back downstairs to the main level. We both suspected perhaps one or both of the original spinster sisters still wandered around, especially on the second floor. I sat on the floor in the middle of the living room and began to explore the house in my mind. I already knew which room contained a ghost. An upstairs bedroom on the southwest corner of the house had windows on two sides and a door with a window in it that led to a small balcony. In spite of the windows, the room was very dark.

I checked all the rest of the house before I entered this room. The rest of the house was clear. Once I was sure of that, I went into the dark room. I was expecting an elderly lady, or perhaps a younger version of one of the spinster sisters who were the original owners.

To my surprise, cowering in a corner of the room, was a man. He had dark hair that was parted in the middle, with a slight wave to it. It had what I think was pomade to hold it in place. I vaguely remember a small mustache. He wore a pair of pleated slacks that were held up by thin suspenders. His white shirt was adorned with a string bow tie. A jacket draped over a chair next to him. He looked to be in his late thirties or early forties. He had a slender build and wasn't much taller than I am. I saw fear in his eyes when he noticed me.

"I won't hurt you," I said.

He didn't move.

"Why haven't you crossed over?" I asked, hoping a little conversation would put him at ease.

"I'm afraid," he said.

"Why are you afraid?"

"If I go through that light, I'll go straight to Hell."

I smiled. "No, you won't," I said. "There is no such thing as Hell."

"You sure about that?" I could see he wasn't going to be an easy sell.

"Yes, I am very sure," I said.

Then he surprised me. He stood up and reached for me. I hugged him without thinking about what I was doing. The man cried for a very long time. When he ran out of tears, he turned to the light and walked into it. I thought I saw a hand reach down to welcome him. A grin spread over his face and all disappeared. I would have very much liked to hear his story.

I got some of it when I announced to my friend that the house was now clear. She told me I had been sitting in the living room for over forty-five minutes. I thought it had been maybe five, ten minutes at the most. She also said she knew I had done the work because she felt as though the sun came out inside the house. Everything brightened and became more cheerful inside, even though it was pouring rain outside.

It was then she told me more of the history of the house. We had both decided, early on, I wasn't to know too much of its history so that what I found could be validated. She had researched all four of the previous owners. The second owner was a lawyer. He had had some dealings with less than honest folk while living in the house. Rumor had it, that he slept with a gun under his pillow. Apparently, he had dealings with nefarious individuals at some point in his life. He installed bars on all the windows, which my friend had taken off when she moved in. There must have been something that he had personally done that brought him a feeling of guilt. It frightened him so much that when it came time to cross over, he refused.

When her friends came to visit, they wanted to know what she had done to the house. It was so bright and cheerful.

22

Grief

*The actuality of death and the experience of grief
sinks in at different times for everyone.*

VALERIE ORR

I have struggled with this chapter for many reasons. At first, I put it off because I thought I had not had much experience with grief. I decided to interview a friend who has had many experiences with grief. While en route to his house, it dawned on me I had been blocking out my one experience with grief that tore me apart.

At one point in my life, I lost everything: a beautiful home, my job, my self-esteem, and worst of all, custody of my children. Some would call my experience the dark night of the soul. Maybe. For me, it was so gut-wrenchingly painful, I nearly died from it. I got to the point where I didn't really care whether I lived or died. I hoped death would provide an oblivion to comfort me from my grief. That didn't happen. Life kept me breathing, like it or not.

When grief comes from the death of a loved one it can be just as devastating. You feel like a part of you has been torn loose never to return again. With that action, you can feel as though you have been violated. There is the feeling that God has somehow reached into your heart and taken away something very precious, and it cannot be replaced.

It doesn't always help to know that your loved one is happy on the other side. The sense of loss overrides everything. The companionship is just not the same, even when you hold that person in your heart.

No two people experience grief in the same way. There is no good/bad, or right/wrong way to do it. Not only that, but it differs with each person making a transition as no two relationships are the same.

Some pass it over almost as though nothing happened, and yet find they have trouble sleeping or seem prone to colds and other diseases. Others take years and some never fully recover. Lost in their grief they lose sight of the world around them. The joy of life leaves them cold and alone.

In observing people during the grieving process, I find

those who experience their grief in all its forms heal more quickly. It's as if they explore all of their grief until there is nothing left. At that point, they are ready to get on with their lives. It's the people who try to ignore their grief and pretend everything is all right that are often most troubled in the long run.

For some the grief takes the form of "What do I do now?" Often a spouse or partner shines when it comes to nitpicky details like doing the taxes. The one left behind has no clue as to how to do that.

The loss of a parent can be difficult. Grief has to be put aside because of all the legal nonsense and paperwork required of various agencies. Federal taxes, state taxes and other problems rear their ugly heads.

Even worse are the fights between siblings over what the deceased left behind. Siblings who were loving and kind to each other suddenly become jealous or greedy about their share of the leavings. The departed are on their way to peace and love while their heirs are so busy fighting they forget to grieve until long after it is all over. Not only do those left behind grieve the loss of the loved one, but now they have the added grief of being separated from their family and even friends.

I think the most difficult loss comes from the death of a child. Children are supposed to outlive their parents. I have yet to meet a parent who has lost a child and recovers from the loss without feelings of helplessness and emptiness. The loss is deep and frequently accompanied by self-recrimination. So often parents think there must have been something they could have done to prevent the death from happening. Not only do they grieve the loss, but they add guilt to the mix.

Which leads me to the question: just what is grief? According to Webster's Dictionary the definition of grief is "a deep and poignant distress caused by or as if by bereavement." Of course, that definition meant I needed to look up *bereavement*. That had a more clear-cut definition: "the loss of a loved one by death." To simplify all that, I would say that grief is the pain following the death or loss of a loved one. Divorce can be just as painful.

While it may ease the mind of a grieving person to know that their loved one is experiencing peace and love, it doesn't mean much. The one who crossed over is gone, never to return again. The emptiness inside cannot be filled.

There are things a grieving person can do to ease the loss. Talking to the loved one as if they are there helps a lot. Meditation and quiet listening may bring a feeling of the lost loved one being near. Which is real, by the way. Most people who cross over are deeply concerned about grieving loved ones. They want to bring comfort and don't know how. They are aware of the anguish and the tears. Some become so concerned they stay as ghosts, so they can be near the grieving person to try to help comfort them.

You can sense or hear people who have crossed over in your own heart. Sometimes it's just a feeling of warmth, or that everything will work out. Other times there may be an actual communication and the person left behind has a sudden inkling of where the deed has been placed, or they find they remember where the key to the safety deposit box was put. There is simply a feeling that the loved one is with you, and it feels comforting.

Frequently, the person who crosses over has no thought for those left behind. That happens more often than not. I sensed a lot of joy and celebration at my grandfather's funeral, but I never heard a word from him. I have not had a sense of his presence. He is gone. We were very close to each other as I grew up, and I have missed him very much.

I talked to my father for several months after he made his transition, and then one day I noticed he wasn't around anymore. He had moved on. I still sense him once in a while, but we don't talk now. I miss him, too.

What people forget is that this life is but a mere minisecond in the eons of time. More often than not, the person who has made a transition is waiting for friends and loved ones when it is their turn. The lights do not go out. The loved one doesn't just disappear forever. Death is a part of life. It allows us to move on to new adventures. We may return and spend other lives with the same loved ones. The separation is not permanent.

People tend to reincarnate in groups. The same people interact with each other during many lifetimes. In one lifetime, a person may be a father with a daughter. In another lifetime they may switch roles, or they may decide to simply be friends. So many times, I have met someone, seemingly for the first time, and yet I feel like I have known them all my life.

Guides are often a part of the group. In one lifetime, I can play the role of a guide for someone I love, and in another that person plays the guide. It is one reason why we are comfortable with our guides. They are good friends, too.

Continuing on in this lifetime without the aid and comfort of a loved one may seem daunting. It helps to know you will be reunited, although, it may not help with everyday life issues. The emptiness of their not being present in the flesh is a natural feeling. However, no one is truly alone.

We are here to help each other. I have repeatedly asked Oreg why we have trouble healing ourselves, be it from illness, pain, or grief. His answer is always the same. "We are not meant to heal alone."

We have each other. We not only learn from each other, we care for one another. Even strangers become wonderful saviors in times of stress and disasters. Floods, fires, storms, and wars have a way of bringing us together. It's a big reason why we are here.

While working on this chapter my hairdresser told me a story. That particular day, she was wearing purple. It is not an everyday color for her. Her daughter-in-law had made her transition three years past. During the final stages of her illness, the woman expressed deep concern that people would forget her. A couple of days before she died, the family gathered around and told her they would wear purple and do an act of kindness to commemorate the anniversary of her death. The day my hairdresser told me the story was the third anniversary.

There Is No Hell

I must not fear.
Fear is the mind-killer.
Fear is the little death that brings total obliteration.
I will face my fear. I will permit it to pass over me
and through me. And when it has gone past,
I will turn the inner eye to see its path.
Where the fear has gone there will be nothing.
Only I will remain.

FRANK HERBERT

23

There Is No Hell

Too many people are thinking of security instead of opportunity. They seem to be more afraid of life than death.

JAMES F BYRNES

I am sorry to disappoint you. There really is no such thing as Hell, unless you self-impose it on yourself while still living here on Earth. I know, this is a big disappointment. You really would like there to be such a place in the afterlife for people like Hitler, serial killers and other such unpopular people. Or you may think the uncle, cousin, brother, or co-worker who abused you, should go to Hell. It isn't like that.

Actually, hell somehow derives from *hades*, which is

the Greek word for a garbage dump. The ancient Greeks and neighboring countries of that region burned their garbage because of the smell. Being a warm climate, garbage got pretty odiferous. Prisoners were sent to hades to tend the fires.

Until the Christian era began, the concept of Hell did not exist as we know it today. Dante's *Inferno* made a big deal of it. It was quite popular in its time and is still a popular read today. Christ certainly never mentioned it. However, a few New Testament writers do bring it up. As time went on, Christian leaders found Hell a convenient way to keep their parishioners in line. They even went so far as to make it a sin if you didn't attend church.

I find the origin of the word *sin* interesting too. The King James version of the Bible came up with that word. Mind you, the King James version of the Bible had been through several translations before it got translated into English. Sin is an archery term meaning "missed the mark." In archery contests, an assigned observer would call out "sin" if the arrow did not enter the center circle on a target.

Repent came from a Latin term *metanoia*, vaguely translated as "change your ways or direction." Through the years, church leaders had a great time with these words. Sin became something you did wrong, and thus you needed punishment. Repent became a powerful term causing people to feel such great regret over their actions that they sought ways of atonement. Church officials used sin and repent as symbols of power to control their parishioners. They succeeded.

Then some religions came up with the lovely idea of tithing which means donating ten percent of your income to the church or synagogue. Some factions have made it a sin if you don't tithe. I know of a few that actually require you to show your tax returns to the powers that be, to prove you have tithed the full amount. Ahem.

We humans have a delightful way of making life difficult for each other. It is what makes the world go 'round, so to speak. If we didn't mess with each other, life would be terribly boring. You disagree? Well, then why do you like to read books and watch movies where the heroes and heroines have to solve terrible, often violent, problems? Why are mysteries so popular? Historical fiction is a very popular genre where the characters undergo sorrowful tragedies and live through gruesome wars and other such events. We humans love to watch movies where the characters get caught up in all kinds of violent events, the more detailed the better.

Let's face it. Pollyanna-type stories bore us. One happy event after another is hard to believe, much less hold our interest. We dream of peace. We say we want our lives to be uneventful. We say we long for a time of quiet and rest. If such a period of time comes along, almost certainly, after a short while, we get creative. Things happen, and we are back to longing for peace and quiet again.

So why are we here you may ask? For most of my life that was the number one question. Nobody had an answer for it. Even the various religions leave that question alone. Some hint at answers.

Some factions of the Christian religion say we are to live a good life so we can spend the rest of eternity sitting at the feet of God singing His praises. I don't think it would take very long before God would get bored with that. Sitting at the feet of a supreme being and singing praises for millions of years is not my idea of fun either. And then there are the people who don't sing on key. Do they all sing together? Or does each one sing individually, whatever praise comes to mind, all at the same time? You can imagine what a racket that would make.

Besides, that is placing God in the image of man. Only human beings would conceive of the idea of having people sit at their feet and sing their praises. Our egos love praise. The Bible says we were created in the image of God. I think we created God in the image of man.

I cannot imagine God being an angry and vengeful being. I also do not think God is up there in the sky somewhere, sitting on a cloud, and acting like Santa Claus by putting us on a naughty or nice list.

Whole religions have been based around the idea of karma. If you are bad in one life, the next life will make you a victim of the wrongful doings of the first life. A few religions say that you will continue to reincarnate until everything you have done in all your lifetimes has come into balance. Then you may move on to Nirvana, or Heaven, or some other pleasant place to live in peace and harmony for all eternity.

I disagree. It takes a very advanced soul to come in and create the events like Hitler did. The same is true for some of his aides. However, no one in recent history has brought to human consciousness the awareness of atrocities that Hitler has. Instead of ignoring genocide, the media now reports it in detail. Hate crimes have become headlines for news reports. People all around the Earth are crying out for change. We want peace. Very few understand it is a matter of individual choice.

Once he transitioned, Hitler was set apart from the general population. He needed to heal himself. Oreg says he is still in isolation. Other healers are working with him. You may not think he deserves it. You are okay in feeling that way.

I had a surprising experience at an air show recently.

At the end of the show, a WWII plane flew past followed by the most up-to-date jet the government is willing to show the public. On the first pass, I saw the heavens open up and a host of angels filled the sky. On the second pass of the two planes, in ones and twos, ghost planes flew into formation behind them. By the third pass, the sky was filled with ghost planes of all ages, from the beginning of the first plane ever built to current time. Some were familiar and some I had never seen the likes of before.

I asked Oreg what was happening. He explained that most of the planes were flown by pilots who had died in combat. Some were flown by test pilots. The angels had come to honor them.

"Why?" I asked.

"They were willing to take risks others wouldn't even consider," he answered.

"What makes pilots so special, then? Other people take risks."

"Yes. They are honored when the opportunity arises."

"Does this happen at every air show?" I asked.

"No," he answered.

"Why now?" I had noticed the crowd had grown quiet. Some even had their hands over their hearts. I knew they weren't seeing what I was seeing, but somehow sensed something reverent was occurring.

"The participants are all available. This event has happened before in other times. However, between the crowd watching, the participants here, the hosts of beings in the sky, and the few people in the crowd who, like you, can see what is happening, have not been able to come together like this before. It is a great happening."

"Huh," I said. I am not sure I understand all of this yet. I am still working on it. Sometimes the answers seem too simple.

Getting back to Hell, I have yet to hear of an afterlife experience, including my own, that involved Hell. According to my guides, serial killers and other villains spend a period of time separate from the rest of the population just as Hitler has. During this experience, they have time to recuperate from their earthly experiences. It is more like recovering from a long illness. Healing occurs during this time. Once they have recovered, they go back into circulation again and may eventually reincarnate. Most often the next life is very different from the difficult life of being a killer or rapist, etc. Sometimes they end up as the victim just to learn both sides of the event.

I admit I have no real understanding about the constant need for war on this planet. It seems to be a very ingrained part of the earthly experience. It is a very intense effort. Rulers make up reasons for the wars, and young men and women blindly follow. The many peacemakers also work intensely trying to prevent war and to encourage love and acceptance of others in spite of differences in religions and ways of doing things. Both parties have lessons to learn, experiences to be enjoyed (or not).

Somewhere along my timeline, I asked Oreg other questions that bothered me.

"Why do we die, if we are going to be reborn again?" was the first question.

"It's like reading a book," he said. "Once you have finished the story it is time to try another one."

"Why can't we be more like a series of stories using the same characters? Dying seems, well, so permanent."

"You each have a limited number of experiences to bring to each other. A new set of characters offers fresh experiences and different personalities. You do not carry the same personality with you for each lifetime."

"Does that mean we forget everything we learn in this lifetime and then die and have to do it all over again?

"Not necessarily. Once you have studied your current lifetime, you decide what you are going to retain and use in the next lifetime. Nothing is lost. Nothing is forgotten. Wisdom from other lifetimes may also be useful in what you want to do in the next life. It's up to you each time."

"Am I alone in my decisions?

"You have mentors on the other side of the veil who will help you if you ask for it."

"I do? Are you one of my mentors?" This was a new idea for me.

"We have worked together for many lifetimes. Sometimes you serve as a mentor for others and I help you with that when you ask."

I grew uncomfortable at this point. "What do you mean I mentor people?"

"This is not an ego thing," was his first reply as though reading my mind. "More experienced souls may choose to be guides for others during their lifetimes. You can even be a guide for more than one soul. You may want to experience being a guide and then switch back to having another life. The choices are endless."

"Huh," (My word for I am not too sure about this.) "This is so far apart from the world religions. None of them teach what you are telling me."

"Of course not," he said. "The purpose of religion is to provide a path for study. Religions are manmade."

"I doubt my minister would agree with that," I said.

"Maybe not. But don't shortchange him. He may not share everything he knows with his congregation, knowing they aren't ready to hear everything."

"Point made," I said. "I don't share everything I know

either. I have another question, changing the subject. Why is old age so difficult? Why do we suffer so much as we get older?"

Oreg laughed. "If you felt good, would you be willing to die?"

"I have heard some people are."

"You have choice again. Some people like a quick exit so they can get on with things. Others like to check out slowly, savoring the experience. Some, like your mother, fight it every step of the way. The body has to forcibly shut down bit by bit to encourage her to transition."

"She is having a rough time of it. Thankfully, she isn't in pain."

"That is one reason why she is taking her time. She doesn't feel rushed. She is working through her own agenda. Be patient with her."

I still didn't get the point. "So why all the suffering?" I asked. "Cancer, for example, can be ugly in so many ways."

"Souls whose bodies suffer from these diseases certainly don't want to stick around for a long time. It is their indication it is time to go home and most do so quite willingly."

"What about those who don't?"

"You already know what happens."

"You mean ghosts?

"Sometimes. Or the pain of living either physically or emotionally gets to be too much and they let go of their bodies and go home."

"Huh."

You can believe what you want. I have no desire to change your religion or any of your beliefs. That is not what this book is about. As a healer, I have been present at the time of final transition for many people. It is an awesome experience filled with both magnificence and sorrow.

Trust me, once people make their transition, there is no sorrow for them. The sorrow remains in the people left behind. For the people making the transition, it is time to go home. It is a time for celebration and great rejoicing.

Everything in this book is true. Or not. Even for me, these thoughts are not carved in stone. Yet, somehow, I find comfort in what I have learned. I have stopped seeking for the meaning of life and why we are here. I have come to accept that the answers to my questions change as my awareness changes.

We come here on purpose, but not necessarily with purpose. Sometimes we come in sharing agreements with others over situations we would like to experience while here. Such opportunities are not available on the other side. Once here, we can do anything we want. We can experience tragedy, a broken heart, true love, war, a difficult illness, and work out problems with other people. The list is endless and as varied as there are people on the planet.

It can be a lot of fun here. It's up to you. You have total responsibility for your own life. You can be happy, sad, or frustrated. You can regret your actions or learn from them. You may be responsible *to* another person if you choose, but you are never responsible *for* another person's life. As someone said, "You may as well be yourself. Everyone else is taken."

I am often asked how do I manage to live in such a stressful world and not be influenced by it. Oh, but I do. I often get caught up in my stuff. I flounder around for a while until I get bored or remember who I am. As soon as I remember that I, and I alone, am responsible for everything that comes into my life, I can also remember that I am free to change any part of it.

Attitude is always the first thing needing change. How I see things determines my point of view. I can choose to stay all caught up in current events, family problems, an unhappy marriage, or a job I hate. By changing my attitude, I am free to see things differently. Sometimes that is all that is needed. Or it opens windows I thought were closed and I can actually change my living situation, job, or even my marriage. Every problem comes with a solution, often several. A friend of mine once commented she had a teacher who said, "There are no problems, only solutions that aren't working." I chuckled over that idea.

It's easy really. I just do the work that is placed in front of me. It is enough. I no longer am troubled by politics, tragedies, and death. I see no reason to worry about things and events over which I have no control. When a problem, event, or even a tragedy appears in my life, I deal with it as best I can and move on. I have that choice and I use it.

Life is good and I love being a part of it.

And the reason for why we are here?

Because we want to be.

It is our choice.

24

A Late Addition

Just when I thought I had finished the book, I was given a gift. I had been working with a client suffering from amyotrophic lateral sclerosis (ALS), commonly called Lou Gehrig's disease. We worked together for several months until he decided to discontinue treatment shortly before he made his transition.

We did have some discussions on the meaning of life and what happens in the afterlife. One discussion in particular was quite heated. I will not go into what he believed, because that is breaking confidentiality, and I promised him I would not do that. I did share with him much of what I have written in this book. He disagreed with me.

He made his transition a few days later. I heard about it the following day. I meditated about it for a while. I felt some human feelings of sadness as I knew I would miss him. He was a very good friend, and I took much delight in working with him. I knew my client had been welcomed home with ceremony and rejoicing. I could feel his happiness at being home.

Just when I thought I might be imagining this, he popped into my head. I could see him quite clearly and he was grinning from ear to ear.

"I thought you would like to know you're right," he said.

That's all he said. I felt like he wanted to validate all that I have written, but he didn't know about the book. Then I realized he was talking about our conversations, and my points of view concerning why we are here. Once I got that, he left.

Wow!

Also by Linnie Thomas

The Encyclopedia of Energy Medicine

The *Encyclopedia of Energy Medicine* presents complete information on the practical applications of biofield therapies of both Eastern and Western origin. While other encyclopedias discuss chakras, meridians, and the energy field, this book goes much deeper. It also includes information on how you can pursue an exciting career in complementary and integrative medicine.

Laws Governing Energy Medicine Practitioners

If you don't know the laws governing touch in your state or jurisdiction, you and your practice might be vulnerable to prosecution. This comprehensive guidebook explains the difference between licensure and certification while providing a thorough overview of the legal requirements for both touch and counseling for all fifty states, the District of Columbia, Puerto Rico, Guam, and Canada.

About the Author

Linnie Thomas is the award-winning author of two best-selling books about healing: *The Encyclopedia of Energy Medicine* and *Laws Governing Energy Medicine Practitioners*.

A Certified Spiritual Healer and Diplomat of Earth Stewardship, Assembly of Spiritual Healers and Earth Stewards, she is now a full-time author, student, and instructor in the healing, metaphysical, and spiritual fields.

Linnie holds certification as both a practitioner and as an instructor with Healing Touch Program™. She has studied more than one hundred biofield therapies and conducts workshops and lectures about the biofield and also medical intuition.

Visit her online at www.linniethomas.com.

Made in the USA
Columbia, SC
21 October 2018